Becoming Iris Murdoch

Becoming Iris Murdoch

Frances White

Series Editor: Peter J. Conradi, FRSL

Kingston University Press
SHORT BIOGRAPHY SERIES

Kingston University Press
Kingston University
Penrhyn Road
Kingston-upon-Thames
Surrey, KT1 2EE

British Library Cataloguing in Publication Data available.
ISBN: 978-1-899999-60-6

Published as part of the KUP Short Biography Series.

Series Editor, KUP Short Biography Series:
Peter J. Conradi, FRSL

Set in: Baskerville 10pt/12pt
Printed in the UK by Lightning Source.

Produced by:
Shabana Ansari
Victoria Burton
Abena Hagan
Chantelle Harbottle
Gillian Pimm
Meike Sohner
Zsofia Verhas
Richard Wood

Cover Image: NPG x 26364
Iris Murdoch by Madame Yevonde.
bromide print on velvet card mount, 1967
© Yevonde Portrait Archive

For Stephen,
Samuel, Charles,
& Alistair

Frances White was born in London. As a small child she lived in Japan where she discovered reading. From then on she lived in books. Semi-educated at various schools, she talked her way into Hertford College, Oxford to read English, and briefly taught before turning towards libraries.

After an M.A. in Librarianship at Loughborough University she did research for the British Library then retreated to rural Ireland where she kept goats and began a PhD on Iris Murdoch at Queen's University, Belfast. This was abandoned in favour of motherhood, hens, geese, pigs and gardening.

However, her misspent youth reading Iris Murdoch caught up with her in the end and at the age of fifty - a late bloomer - she finally gained a PhD from Kingston University for a thesis on Murdoch's work, written whilst working as a cashier and horticultural buyer for the local supermarket. Married for over thirty years to Stephen White, an Anglican priest and theologian, she has two teenage sons.

'It is high time that such an accomplished Murdoch scholar paid attention to these formative years, for it is here that one finds not only deep emotional upheaval, but also the heady continental intellectualism that intoxicated Iris Murdoch – and wrought a unique figure in twentieth-century British Letters.'

Anne Rowe, Associate Professor in English Literature
Director, the Iris Murdoch Archive Project

Contents

Introduction

How do I write a Biography of Iris Murdoch as *I* Know Her?

Biography is by nature the most universally profitable, universally pleasant of all things: especially Biography of distinguished individuals.

Thomas Carlyle

Becoming *Iris Murdoch* is an account of a critically formative period in the life of the young woman who was born Jean Iris Murdoch on 15 July 1919 at 59, Blessington Street, Dublin, and who by the time she died of Alzheimer's on 22 February 1999 in Oxford, had become the writer Iris Murdoch, Dame of the British Empire, her iconic portrait by Tom Phillips hanging in the National Portrait Gallery. This short biography seeks to uncover key moments, experiences and people in the process of her intellectual, spiritual and emotional journey towards identifying and achieving her life ambitions. A secondary aim of this book is more personal: it seeks to explore in an open fashion a factor in biography writing which is always necessarily present but often ignored – the relationship between biographer and biographee. So the tone of this work is deliberately personal: this single vision of Iris Murdoch, which does not pretend to catholicity or impartiality, is mine.

Biography is culture specific[1]

Three factors encourage me to boldness in this venture. First, the rubric of Kingston University Press's invitation to try one's novice hand at biography writing, as this overtly values the 'increase in "personal voice scholarship"', fosters 'the development of new and innovative ways to approach biographical writing', and recognizes 'that contemporary biographical work may concentrate solely on one section of a life, may focus exclusively on an overlooked or forgotten area of the subject's endeavour or may indeed be a hybrid form which crosses the apparent boundaries of memoir and biography'.[2]

Second, as a single research foray into the unknown activity of biography writing I spent a day in the British Library reading (with great enjoyment) *Biography: Writing Lives* by Catherine Neal Parke, and I want to share my rich loot from that book. Parke offers a 'self-evident poetics of biography, a poetics inseparable from the genre' because it is 'the secretary to our existence' (fine phrase), and observes that 'readers' interest in this genre might also seem to share similar qualities of the self-evident' (Parke, xiii). This interest is closely related to the passion for fiction (my own area of expertise) because biography 'rivals fiction in its imaginative appeal to the powerful emotions of hope and fear, desire and hate, attraction and repulsion, as well as for the fact that in its long history biography has identified issues and tackled problems endemic to life, which are in equal measure practical, metaphysical, quotidian, and mysterious, and which nearly every age, to date, has felt the obligation to rethink' (Parke, xiii). Indeed I find as one grows older biography overtakes the appeal of fiction; real people are so much quirkier and more fascinating than any fictional character – even one of Iris Murdoch's.

Parke's questions about matters that 'motivate biographical research' also resonate with me (why do I want to try to write this book when I have a thousand other projects shrieking for my attention?). She itemizes them (and I parenthetically respond, according to motivation level) thus:

1. 'How and why did a particular person do what she did, think what she thought, imagine what she imagined?' (Yes)
2. 'How did the person's private and public lives relate to and influence one another?' (Yes)
3. 'How did childhood affect the adult life?' (No)
4. 'To what degree is the subject conscious of various shaping forces?' (Yes)
5. 'How did cultural and historical events affect that life?' (Yes)
6. 'How may these elements, organized as a pattern by the biographical narrative, serve, in turn, to account

for and explain a particular life and the forms it
took?' (Yes)

7. 'What makes one life more worth writing about than
another?' (Like Virginia Woolf I am not sure that this
is so.)

8. 'How and why does a particular biographer choose a
particular biographical subject?' (*Yes*. Very much yes.)

In one sense for me the answer is obvious: Iris Murdoch
is what I do. In another way it is very obscure to me *why*
Iris Murdoch *is* what I do – question four above seems
to be as applicable to the biographer as to her subject, a
matter on which I do not choose to dwell overmuch.

I was fascinated to learn that 'over the past 200 years,
professional writers have surpassed the former leading
candidates of biographical interest in Western culture:
royalty, saints, and military heroes', that 'writers,
beginning in the late seventeenth century, became the
new heroes of modern print culture and expanding
literacy' and that 'their lives also became templates for
post-Renaissance notions of the relation between public
and private self, the Western invention of individual
identity, and the foundational concept of the reality of a
psychological life' (Parke, xvii), especially as her ensuing
remark seems irrefutable: 'authors might seem to be
among the least likely candidates for biography, given
how much time they must spend alone' (Parke, xviii).
And I was given to think by the idea that 'biography is
not a monolithic term' and that 'there are various ways
to divide up this generic territory' (Parke, 29). Parke
offers two possible taxonomies of biography (another fine

phrase). 'One way is to discriminate among:

1. Popular biographies narrating the lives of current celebrities
2. Historical biographies emphasizing their central and influential figures' relations to and effects on their times
3. *Literary biographies recreating the life and personality of artists, attempting to account for the particular bent of their talent and sometimes, as in critical biographies, interpreting and assessing their work*
4. Reference biographies, also called collective biographies,
5. Fictional biographies taking factual materials about real people and events and developing them by applying fictional narrative techniques.' (Peake, 29)[3]

The second taxonomy 'identifies categories conceived more explicitly from the writer's point of view regarding the practice of biography, including the relative proportions of attempted subjectivity and objectivity, the kinds of research involved, and the respective proportions of artful imagination and historical fact:

1. The "objective" biography which, though it cannot entirely omit subjective choices (even the ordering of data involves personal decisions) attempts to keep them to a minimum
2. The "scholarly-historical" biography, characterized by the "careful use of selected facts, strung together

in chronological order, with some historical background"

3. *The "artistic-scholarly" biography for which the author does all the homework required for the scholarly-historical biography but presents these materials in "the liveliest and most interesting manner possible" while not altering or adding to the facts*

4. The "narrative scholarly-historical" biography for which the author collects all the evidence and "turns it into a running narrative, almost fictional in form", though still not adding material,

5. "Fictional" biography, for which the author relies on secondary sources and treats the life of the historical subject as a novelist would treat a character, adding and inventing as the author sees fit for the effects she is trying to create.'[4]

It is clear to me that my attempt will fall into category three of both taxonomies (which is why I have italicized them above). This book will try to recreate the life and personality of Iris Murdoch, 'attempting to account for the particular bent of her talent,' and although I shall stick to fact rather then veer off into fiction I don't aspire to the 'scholarly-historical' but hope rather to make the young life of Iris Murdoch both lively and interesting. In either case, Parke warns me, 'the biographer's talents and inclination, the imagined audience for the biography, and, to some degree, the qualities of the biographical subject all enter into the writer's choice of research methods and compositional form for a life' (Parke, 29-30).

Well, I wondered, as I drank a cup of Peyton &

Byrne's coffee and communed with Mr Punch on the British Library terrace (if you have never found this, it has a flourishing and fragrant herb garden and is just the place to soothe the headache that comes from trying to read one's entire allotment of books in a single day). Well – before I digressed – I wondered what my 'talents and inclination' as a would-be biographer might be, what 'the imagined audience' for my biography of Iris Murdoch is, and what 'the qualities of the biographical subject' are. Of the first, I was (am) very doubtful; of the second, unsure (though I have since decided); but of the third I have no doubt. She is both Saint and Artist, as well as fully human. (I will come to her shortly.) But what I want to do in writing this book is to look at the part of her life where Iris Murdoch herself was very doubtful of her own 'talents and inclination'.

In this I was encouraged by reading (the only other non-Iris Murdoch book this study will discuss) Alexandra Harris's recently published *Virginia Woolf*.[5] I read this simply because Virginia Woolf is another of the things I do (along with Jane Austen: these three women form a Trinity of Wonder in my pantheon of writers). It was an uncanny experience. Harris was thinking about Virginia Woolf exactly as I was thinking about Iris Murdoch. I went from my own musing about the time when Iris Murdoch had no job, no money, no husband, and had written no book, to reading – and it is worth quoting this in full as it exactly parallels my own thinking:

In 1907 Virginia Woolf was twenty-five and not yet a published novelist [....] She did not know whether

15

she would marry and have a family. It was not at all clear whether she would prove herself a genius, or merely quite good [....] She went on to become one of the greatest writers of all time. Today she is celebrated not only for her novels but for her essays, her social polemics, her memoirs, her experiments in biography, her glittering and moving diaries, and her many many letters. The story of her life is one of determination, hard work, and untiring interest in the world around her [....] Reading chronologically through Woolf's diaries and letters, it is possible to put hindsight temporarily on hold and appreciate the decisions she made day by day [....] We can flick ahead and see that she will recover from a breakdown and finish a masterpiece, but Woolf's remarkable toughness and tenacity become more apparent when we remember that she, of course, could not. (Harris, 7-8)

Iris Murdoch lived a very different life in a very different world from Virginia Woolf. But she too suffered deep grief and came close to breakdown, and she exhibits the same combination of self-belief and self-doubt that Harris identifies in Virginia Woolf's early life. I am struck, like Harris, by trying to imagine what it felt like to Iris Murdoch *then*, when she did not know what she would become, whether she would marry, whether she would prove herself a genius etc. She too went on to become one of the greatest writers of all time.

The biographee

The world of Iris Murdoch studies is expanding geographically and deepening through the calibre of scholars engaging with her work.[6] On my first attempt to write a thesis on her novels at Queen's University Belfast, doubt was expressed as to whether she was a large enough sole subject for a monograph – 'had you not better compare her with Muriel Spark?' Even back in 1989, substantial secondary and tertiary literature on her work existed: this has more than doubled in the past quarter of a century. I have made a small contribution to the detailed picture Iris Murdoch scholarship is building up – polished a few tiny tiles to set into the glittering mosaic formed by the whole. But I don't want to write a formal literary biography here, nor a psychoanalytic one delving into Iris Murdoch's childhood and complexes – not only out of respect for her own mistrust of that 'road',[7] but out of full agreement with her that it sheds little and dubious light. Rather, I want to try to get a feel for the ineluctable happenstances of her life and aspects of her personality which lead to the pivotal choices she made and which will offer a sense of what compelled her to make them.

To that end I want to focus on a critical decade in Iris Murdoch's life – or to be precise a critical eleven years – from August 1945 when, aged twenty-six, she was sent by UNRRA (the United Nations Relief and Rehabilitation Administration) to work in refugee camps in Europe to August 1956, when, aged thirty-seven, she married John Bayley. The experiences of those years were formative: they shaped the whole of Iris Murdoch's career and achievements. She was multi-talented and could have followed many paths. She became a novelist and a moral philosopher, but she was tempted by and tentatively explored other ways of life. Each chapter of this biography, framed within those years, teases out one strand of the potential which the young Iris Murdoch discovered within herself. She might have been a great political activist. She might have been one of the world's great mistresses; her sexual imbroglios leave the exploits of her own characters – even in her famed bedroom farce, *A Severed Head* (1961) –in the shade. (She dreamt of being the mother of a large family.) She can be imagined as the wise head of a religious order, like her own Abbess in *The Bell* (1958); or as the head of an Oxford or Cambridge College (she was an inspiring teacher). Had Iris Murdoch left art to one side and followed her philosophical bent she would have become even more of a philosopher to be reckoned with than she already is. But in the end, art won. Art can do things which philosophy cannot, and, though torn between them, it is through literature that Iris Murdoch has made the greatest impact.

Mixed reasons for this, some internal (caused by her own priorities and drives), and some external (caused by the accidents of history and her own wayward behaviour), emerge in this portrait of that crucial decade. But a greater trajectory in Iris Murdoch's life subsumes each conflicting ambition and desire. She wanted to be good. The Good is at the heart of her whole endeavour. Why (and indeed how) we should become good is central to her moral philosophy. How we do (or mostly don't) become good underpins the tragi-comedy of her novels which, despite being situated in the strangely unworldly milieu of Murdochland, deal with the human condition, moral and spiritual.

Iris Murdoch felt it was important for novels to have something for everybody and wanted hers to reach all possible readers. She succeeded. Not only is critical study of her work, both literary and philosophical, burgeoning, but she continues to appeal to the 'common reader'. People are discussing her novels on Twitter and book clubs are reading them together. International Iris Murdoch conferences held biennially at Kingston University, London, have a rare flavour as delegates come from both within and without the academy – a mixed bag of professionals and fans. This book embraces such a broad perspective: as well as writing for the already converted, scholars and readers always avid to learn more about her, I want to engage with newcomers to Iris Murdoch for whom I hope this will serve as an appetite-whetting introduction which will lead them to read her work for themselves. Further still, I want to engage with all readers interested in how a person *becomes* that particular person and especially how a writer becomes *that* particular writer, through the choices, decisions, and happenstances of her life.

This is therefore a passionate book, not a dry detached assessment. Partly because I want to share my own passion for Iris Murdoch's work, and partly because she is so passionate herself, about art, ideas, places, people, indeed *life*. It is not an iconoclastic book but nor is it hagiographical. Neither is it over-solemn because she herself was not. Iris Murdoch's fiction is full of self-mockery. In her philosopher characters (Marcus Fisher in *The Time of the Angels*, Rupert Foster in *A Fairly Honourable Defeat*, even John Robert Rosanov in *The Philosopher's Pupil*) she pokes fun at her own philosophical endeavours and it is with tongue in cheek that she opens *Nuns and Soldiers* with 'Wittgenstein —'. No one parodies Iris Murdoch better than she does herself through the novelist character Arnold Baffin in *The Black Prince*. Iris Murdoch takes many things – art, religion, ethics – seriously, but she does not take herself over-seriously, as humility is one of her chief characteristics and she is unconcerned with her image, never seeking to be a 'celebrity' figure.

The biographer

This work is written by an obsessive Iris Murdoch reader (once described as a 'Murdoch anorak' by a professionally-minded academic) who is belatedly turning her private passion into shared scholarship within the international world of Iris Murdoch studies. I don't want to burden readers with scholarly apparatus on this occasion. Dates and details can always be looked up elsewhere for anyone who needs to know them. I shall follow the example set by the young Jane Austen who announced 'Tho' I do not profess giving many dates, yet [...] I think it proper to give some and shall of course make choice of those which it is most necessary for the Reader to know'.[8] Biographical study of Iris Murdoch has begun: Peter J. Conradi did the stone-breaking work in his authorized *Iris Murdoch: A Life*; A.N. Wilson contributed his scurrilous but also insightful personal memoir, *Iris Murdoch as I Knew Her* in revenge for having had the position of authorized biographer taken from him and given to Conradi instead; Valerie Purton has provided a vital critical tool in *An Iris Murdoch Chronology*; David Morgan has offered a provocative and intimate memoir in *With Love and Rage: A Friendship with Iris Murdoch* which focuses on the period of Iris Murdoch's life when she was teaching at the Royal College of Art in London, and Priscilla Martin and Anne Rowe have spun her life and work together in their scholarly but highly readable *Iris Murdoch: A Literary Life*.[9] So why am I writing another?

I have some sixteen biographies of Virginia Woolf on my bookshelves. My unliterary father is bemused: 'But you *know* what happened in her life: how can you read it all *again*?' But one is never reading it again. Each account of a life is a synthesis of the subject and the reader/writer: Julia Briggs's Virginia Woolf is different from Hermione Lee's which is different again from Alexandra Harris's.

What they have in common is immersion in the world and work of Woolf. Just so, my Iris Murdoch is not Conradi's or Wilson's, Morgan's, Martin's or Rowe's. She grows out of my personal encounter with her, out of my forty years of immersion in her fiction and philosophy. Iris Murdoch, whom I only met once (an encounter which I will tell you about later) was my teacher. Through her I have met others who have become my teachers, Jean Paul Sartre, Raymond Queneau, Simone Weil, Ludwig Wittgenstein. She has given me a do-it-yourself philosophy course: slowly, in order to follow what she was telling me in her own books and to find out what her allusions to these philosophers implied, I have read (a little) Plato, Kant, Schopenhauer and others. She also opened up to me the world of art. I visited (and constantly revisit) the galleries where the paintings she embeds in her novels and which are central to her ethical vision, hang. This developed into finding my own special works of art which mean to me what those paintings meant to her. And she gave me London, her own special sense of London. Cheryl Bove has traced all the streets, pubs, buildings and monuments which appear in Murdoch's fiction and provided maps for walks in the book she and Anne Rowe wrote together, *Sacred Space, Beloved City: Iris Murdoch's London*.[10] These maps are a great resource but I was already doing this as a teenager, looking for just where Jake swam in the Thames and where Peter Pan's statue hides in Kensington Gardens. Iris Murdoch's trail in London intersects with Virginia Woolf's. As I walk along the Embankment of Jake Donaghue in *Under the Net* I meet the ghost of Woolf's Helen Ambrose grieving at leaving her children in the opening scene of *The Voyage Out*. London is a literary palimpsest and changes with each reader-walker: for my brother London is full of Sinclair, for others haunted by Dickens.

The point is that Iris Murdoch has made me who I am. Had my father not given me a copy of *The Unicorn* when I was thirteen or fourteen and said you might enjoy this, my life would have been different. She is of course not the sole influence: had I not read Jane Austen and loved Elinor and Edward, Fanny and Edmund, I might not have married an Anglican clergyman. Writers wreak havoc. They help us form our sense of self-identity. They create us. We do not read and remain unchanged. Books are an insidious, often unnoticed, part of becoming who we are.

Method, Structure and Sources

In these days of academic political correctness much is made of the importance of Methodology – a faux-scientific approach to the arts. This biography wantonly flings methodology to the winds. I am searching out the mystery of the formation of this great writer, and I shall skitter from one aspect of her life to another without regard to strict chronology in so doing. I shall weave back and forth in time, retracing the same ground with differing emphasis in individual chapters.

I shall no doubt draw unconsciously upon all the many books and essays on Iris Murdoch which I have read, heard, re-read, half-remembered or forgotten, but which form the rich mental compost out of which all my thoughts about her grow. More consciously, I shall make use of selected texts: Purton's *Chronology* for checking what happened on occasions when exactitude seems to matter, Conradi's biography, and also John Bayley's first volume of memoirs, *Iris*, which is a rich source of anecdote and reflection.[11]

I acknowledge that there are two schools of thought about these memoirs. One holds that they are spiteful pieces of revenge written by a man jealous of his more intelligent, more famous wife, and getting his own back for her success and for her infidelities when she is no longer able to defend herself; the other that they are a great love story and an appreciation of her unique person and genius. I incline to the latter view, but although I think theirs was the happy marriage they both claimed it to be, an unusual marriage that suited the peculiar needs of these two unconventional people, there is nonetheless great pain woven through John Bayley's memories of his life with Iris Murdoch which seeps through the cracks of his narrative and displays itself in the denials, obsessions and contradictions which score his texts.

I shall also draw upon letters written by Iris Murdoch to Raymond Queneau and Hal Lidderdale during these years, held in the Iris Murdoch Special Collections in the Kingston University Archives. Her letters to Frank Thompson and David Hicks have been edited by Peter J. Conradi and published in *Iris Murdoch: A Writer at War: Letters and Diaries 1939-45*.[12] And, excitingly, Anne Rowe and Avril Horner are currently editing a selection to be published as *Living on Paper: Letters from Iris Murdoch: 1934-1995*, which will be a treasure trove for future critical and biographical writing about Iris Murdoch.[13] Some of the letters from which I shall quote here will be included in that volume. Through her letters, Iris Murdoch is able to recount what happened to her, and how she felt about what was happening to her, as she developed into a novelist and philosopher. Or at least *how she chose to present how she felt* to her individual correspondents – one always has to read between the lines of letters as one does with journals; they are riddled with multi-layered self-consciousness and ensuing ironies. (As Hugo Bellfounder remarks in *Under the Net*, 'I'm not saying precisely what I think, but what will impress you and make you respond'.)[14] Her journals, which could be the richest resource of all, are as yet only partly accessible via Conradi's *Iris Murdoch: A Life*. It is to be hoped that one day, Iris Murdoch scholars will have the full range of biographical materials available to them, as Virginia Woolf scholars have.

Finally, there is always a problem about what to call your subject. Just Iris, which both John Bayley, who was married to her for over forty years, and Peter J. Conradi, who knew her well, use, feels too familiar to me, disrespectful; IM, which Wilson chose for his own use, is ugly; Murdoch is correct for scholarly texts, but lacks the resonance of the full name we see emblazoned on book jackets and which she signed with powerful character, thus:

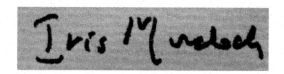

Iris Murdoch she shall be throughout this book, as I want both these inseparable names.

Chapter One

The World: Europe, Sartre and Queneau

Life must be lived forward but understood backwards.

Søren Kierkegaard[15]

The Story So Far

The television series *Miranda* opens with the words, 'Previously in my life …'. Before we plunge into the whirlwind decade which is the focal point of this short biography, we had better see how Iris Murdoch arrived at this point in her development. There will be flash-backs and flash-forwards throughout this narrative, but a sense of her background, childhood, education and early career lays the groundwork for appreciating some formative influences.

Iris Murdoch, born just three years after the 1916 Easter Rising, was the only child of Irish parents, Hughes and Rene (Wills John Hughes Murdoch and Irene Cooper Alice Richardson) who brought her to live in London as a baby – forced out of their homeland by the historical circumstance of the fear engendered by the violence in Ireland during that era. All of these factors remain significant throughout her life and writing. First, her familial isolation which made her create characters in lieu of siblings and gave her a very skewed romanticized mythologized Gothic (I make no apology for adjectival strings – Iris Murdoch is (in)famous for them and refused to be edited) view of the sibling relationship. Second, her Irishness which – again romanticized – was a strong element in her personal myth, and third, her sense of being an exile which gave her empathy with the refugee condition.

She was sent to unconventional schools; first the Froebel Demonstration School as a day pupil and then Badminton School in Bristol as a boarder which made her very lonely – her accounts of whether or not she was happy at school are inconsistent (as I guess would be the case for most of us according to specific recollections and the mood one is in at the time of recalling them). A bright and diligent child, she excelled at these establishments, becoming Head Girl of both schools and winning prizes as well as passing exams and gaining an Open Exhibition to Somerville College, Oxford. Under Beatrice May Baker (BMB), renowned Headmistress, Badminton aspired to progressive internationalism. It charged itself with a citizenship-building role and became a refuge for Jewish girls and *Mischlings* (as partially-Jewish children were known) from Europe. Iris Murdoch was influenced by Badminton's left-wing tendencies to look to the Soviet Union and early developed Communist sympathies.

Oxford and the Second World War coincided in Iris Murdoch's life. She went up in October 1938 and 'from the start [...] led a rather fabulous existence' as Justin Broackes remarks.[16] Just eleven months later, while she was enjoying touring the countryside doing amateur theatricals, England declared war on Germany. (Her diary of that period, 'The Magpie Players – 1939', which paints a colourful picture of the carefree young undergraduate she then was, can be read in *A Writer at War*.) The war had a powerful impact on both her sexual life and intellectual life as we shall see in chapters two and four. She got a first class degree, and then – again forced by the historical times in which she was living – went to work at the Treasury in London. (*A Writer at War* is also an account of her Treasury work; of fire-watching in the Blitz and of the entangled love affairs and Bohemian pub life which formed her experience during those years).

Iris Murdoch had only been abroad once, when she spent ten days at the League of Nations Summer School in Geneva in August 1935; she attended lectures and wrote winning essays on the League of Nations whilst at Badminton. Determined to get out of England and to be actively involved she applied to the United Nations Relief and Rehabilitation Administration (UNRRA) in 1944 and, after a brief period of kicking her heels in their English offices, she got her heart's desire and was sent to Brussels in August 1945, which is where *this* account of her life really begins.

But before we get started (trying to write a biography is a more Tristram Shandyesque experience than I had anticipated – where *does* one begin?) I want to create a governing framework for studying this period in Iris Murdoch's life, dominated by *uncertainty*. We must bear in mind at all times the crucial fact that Harris flags up with regard to Virginia Woolf – *Iris Murdoch does not know what is going to happen to her.* We are reading her life backwards from our present knowledge of her success and stature, with the understanding that Kierkegaard (one of her favourite writers) observes we come retrospectively to obtain: she was living it forwards (as we all do) into the foggy and fearful unknown. I flash forward only in the constant cognizance that Iris Murdoch could not do so.

For Iris Murdoch this was a decade of uncertainty, loneliness, and fear of failure in both work and relationships. In the middle of it she wrote to Queneau:

> I think nothing is really worth anything except (a) being happily married, (b) being a saint, (c) writing a good novel. My chances of (a) diminish yearly, (b) is far too difficult – there remains (c) which still inspires hope. (16 March 1950)

She didn't know of her forty-year marriage to come; she wasn't behaving in a saintly or even (conventionally) moral fashion, and her attempts to publish a novel had so far met with rejection. Furthermore, she was unsure in which directions her talents lay. Not only were they numerous, but her great intelligence was backed up by ferocious powers of concentration, vigorous physical and mental energy and a capacity for sheer hard work. As John Bayley was later to point out:

> A really great artist can concentrate and succeed at almost anything, and Iris would have been no

exception [....] at the Treasury [...] she had made
herself an expert [and] had she concentrated on any
of those careers she could have been a doctor, an
archaeologist, a motor mechanic. (Bayley, 102)

The field of potential was still wide open. She could
pursue the relief work on which she had embarked with
UNRRA. She could return to the Civil Service or to
academia. She could follow a political career. She could
pursue the dream of holiness which haunted her. She
had wanted to be a writer since childhood and stayed
convinced she would write – but what? This axis of
multiple possibilities combined with deep misgivings
is where I am knotting the thread of this biographical
study which has the form of a daisy-stitch in embroidery,
going out at different angles and returning each time
to the central point. I find that biography has parallels
with Iris Murdoch's view of philosophy – adopted from
Kierkegaard – that it 'is like sewing, you must knot the
thread' (*MGM*, 186).

The first thread I am taking up is the effect on Iris
Murdoch of being in Europe and of encountering certain
individuals who were to influence the eventual shape of
her career. Against the grain of the idea already noted in
the Introduction, that authors are unlikely candidates for
biography because they spend so much time alone, this
was a very busy and sociable time in her life. It was also a
time dictated by activism and politics; which accounted
for Iris Murdoch being in Europe. She joined the
Communist party as soon as she got to Oxford – indeed
she once claimed to have been a communist by the time

she was thirteen[17] – and was politically active in London while she worked there. By 1944 she was involved in Labour Party politics despite lacking confidence in the party. And she was deeply concerned with the plight of those displaced by the war.

I have met Jean Paul Sartre!

But her willingness to go and work in the often harsh conditions of the relief camps had unexpected and unforeseeable fringe benefits. She just happened – by this accident of historical timing – to be living in the Rue Neueve in Brussels when Jean Paul Sartre made a brief visit to a conference organized by the Dominicans before going to America to give his famous 1945 speech.[18] Iris Murdoch had already begun to read his novels whilst waiting impatiently in London to be sent abroad. Now, on 24 October 1945, she attended his lecture, taking careful notes in a pale blue, cloth-covered notebook bought for the occasion, which cost her seventy-eight francs.[19] Inside the front cover a gold/red/black/silver sticker says:

100 Ans
Papeteries
NIAS
Bruxelles
1845-1945

And on the first page she inscribed an epigraph from Simone de Beauvoir:

Il nous faut savoir que
nous ne créons jamais pour
autrui que des points de départ
et pourtant les vouloir pour nous
comme des fins.

"*Pyrrhus et Cinéas*"

Iris Murdoch kept that notebook (which she filled with transcriptions and commentaries on works by Sartre) for the rest of her life. The following evening she was present as Sartre held court in a café, where he signed her copy of *L'âge de raison*, '*A Miss Iris Murdoch en sincere homage de JP Sartre, 25.10.45.*'[20] Her excitement bubbles through the letter she wrote to Hal Lidderdale nearly a fortnight later:

I have practically nothing to do and am cynically enjoying myself with the jeunesse dorée, or rather I should say, the jeunesse Sartrienne. Since seeing you I have met Jean Paul Sartre! He came here to give a lecture on existentialism, and I was introduced to him at a select gathering after the lecture, and saw him again at a long Café séance the following day. He is small, simple in manner, squints alarmingly and talks exquisitely. At present I am busily reading everything of his I can lay my hands on. This excitement – I remember nothing like it since the days of discovering Keats and Shelley and Coleridge when I was very young! (6 November 1945)

Sartre might have had a more personal influence on Iris Murdoch had she been able to enter his circle (she would have been putty in his hands as she later was with Elias Canetti). But she did not meet him again; indeed, invited to meet her later when she was writing a book about him, he declined. She would have liked to know Simone de Beauvoir and made a few attempts at getting the chance to do so, but de Beauvoir also rejected her request for a meeting.[21] I will return to the impact that encountering Sartre and her subsequent reading of his philosophy (she bought *L'Etre et le Néant* the following year) was to have on Iris Murdoch's philosophical development and career in chapter four. For now I want to introduce the second French writer who was to hold sway over her, emotionally and intellectually, for the next six years or more, Queneau.

I have a peculiarly clear mental image of the way you looked the very first time I saw you, turning away in the snow down that road in Innsbruck [22]

So Iris Murdoch wrote to Raymond Queneau, novelist, poet, philosopher and member of the mandarin Académie Goncourt, six years after she first met him on 16 February 1946. Queneau was married, established and successful – all she was not, as yet. She already knew his work, having acquired *Pierrot mon ami* the previous summer.[23] One of her ongoing projects during these years was the daunting self-set task of translating the slangy demotic idiosyncratic French of that text – a difficult job even for a trained linguist which Iris Murdoch was not, though she read, wrote and spoke the language well. She fell for Queneau with an unrequited passion that caused her great pain and him much embarrassment. He was captivated to begin with, writing in his journal the day they met: '*Ma traductrice est une fille épatante. Je suis tout de suite séduit. Longue conversation. Nous nous entendons parfaitement*', and '*Adieux – plutôt – tendres*'.[24] I read that with delight on another afternoon in the British Library, experiencing a strange dizzy feeling of surprise that my subject has an objective existence in the minds of others as well as my own; I wonder if that is common to all biographers? Sometimes it feels as if I have made Iris Murdoch up, even though I once met her (and I have not forgotten my promise to tell that story). She even gets a footnote from Queneau's journal editor, making her seem like a bit part in his play, rather than his being a bit part in hers, which is the aspect from which I had viewed him:

> *L'écrivain anglais Iris Murdoch. Elle était une amie et une admiratrice de Queneau et se lança même dans une traduction en anglais de 'Pierrot mon ami' qui n'aboutit pas. Son premier roman publié en 1954, Under the Net, est dédié à R.Q.*[25]

I am *tout de suite séduit* by the French language (as Iris Murdoch was – though it frustrated her to try to express her feelings in it). *Une admiratrice*: how exactly that encapsulates her relationship to Queneau and how much more evocative it is than 'admirer'. And *se lança même dans* – she 'launched herself into' translating *Pierrot*. That gives just the sense of impetuous energy that comes through her letters to him about this endeavour, which, sadly, did indeed *n'aboutit pas*. (I get completely derailed from the tracks of my own biographical project at this point and disappear to re-read *Pierrot mon ami*, *Zazie dans le metro* and *Exercices de style*. I realize that professional biographers must be very self-disciplined, focused people.) This meander down a side-path does however give me a strong sense of why Iris Murdoch fell so in love with Queneau's writings which are as quirky and unique as I'd remembered. 'I can think of no other contemporary writer who touches me as you do, in some lyrical depth where all laughter is tragic' (6 December 1946), she tells him. His mind is 'a country which I find very agreeable' (6 June 1950), and she further admits 'I wish I had a mind like yours. I love and covet your mind as I never have anyone's' (25 October 1950).

Iris Murdoch had yet to discover the richness of her own mind or her own unique narrative voice, as she knows when she tells Queneau, 'You are important to me in all sorts of ways. As a symbol, yes, one instant undiscovered magnetic pole of my own uncertain mind' (24 April 1947). I will return to his influence on the development of her fictional genius in chapter five. But for now, reading Queneau's work also shows me why her attempt to translate him was doomed to failure. When it was rejected, she wrote to him sadly: 'My purely personal disappointment you can imagine. This takes from me something that was very dear to me for many reasons [...] but chiefly I'm sorry to have let you down and been after all unable to produce the goods' (28 November 1946). One of the reasons, however, that the task was dear to her was that the cool clear intellectual exercise of translation gave her mental respite from the heat of the emotional storms she brewed up around her during this period, of which more in chapter two. But it is small wonder that Iris Murdoch recommends the learning of languages as a focus for attention to the world beyond the self – she had personally experienced this means of escaping the voracious demands of the ego.

For despite rare moments of 'ecstatic stillness within and without', which she noted and treasured, this was an emotional roller-coaster of a time for Iris Murdoch, a period of much self-questioning and of loneliness. From Klagenfurt, she wrote to Lidderdale:

> Here life is a mixture of intense boredom (office hours) & the Earthly Paradise (other hours.) [...] I lead an existence of unprecedented peace. In the evening, drinking a pre-prandial beer on the terrace in the sun, and looking away across the lake I feel a most ecstatic stillness within and without. [...] I am writing quite a lot [...] I dream through the day somehow. Immoral, but there it is. (17 April 1946)[26]

And from Graz, she painted a picture of life in the camp for Queneau:

> I am now at Graz working at the studentenheim. I love this camp. Why didn't I come here months ago instead of hanging around in HQs waiting to be promoted? As I cross the 'quad' at evening to check on the accommodation in Barrack V I meet the two Jančars, just back from the university. They are

studying medicine. Under the trees is Pardonjač, one of the philosophers (but not the Pierrot kind) deep in a book. Here comes Elfriede Petek who is an art student and always exquisite tho' she lives in an overcrowded room with 10 other girls. Kamnetsky lounges on the horizon, a problem child, but remember he was in a concentration camp. There is so much life here – quite mysterious to me still, like fishes in a dark aquarium, but very moving and obscurely significant. Most of the students are Yugoslavs, but there are also lots of Poles and Ukraines and some Albanians, White Russians, Lithuanians, Jews various and others. About 300 in all. The main factor in our lives tho' is <u>food</u>. The camp is now on a real starvation diet and my God how can those children study on 200 grammes of bread and one plate of stew and some coffee per day? Improvements soon I hope – but meanwhile heartbreaking [...] (2 June 1946)

Throughout all this, she was steadily reading and writing, and discussing her reading and writing in her letters to friends. She also reveals her moods and vicissitudes, her self-doubts and dogged self-belief, and her loneliness. These features unsurprisingly continued after her return to England in the summer of 1946 to spend a year back at home with her parents in Chiswick, at the age of twenty-seven, penniless and jobless. More surprisingly they persist throughout her year in Cambridge and do not even disappear when she finds a niche back in Oxford with work and friends aplenty.

I want to conclude this first chapter by returning to the knotting point of the thread, Iris Murdoch's own lack of confidence in her future. Her uncertainty and mood-swings are evident in her letters to Lidderdale and Queneau, writing to whom kept her going through this often bleak time, which she herself called 'Nadir' (*IMAL*, 247). At her lowest ebb she wrote to Lidderdale: 'Yesterday, I must say, I felt that the only practical problem now remaining to me was: can one rely on 100 aspirins, or is a tube train safer? Today I think perhaps there are alternatives to instant death, tho' I'm not at all sure what they are' (6 September 1946), and to Queneau: 'I have also been going through a time of particular desolation and difficulty. I regret many things' (15 September 1946). There is a forlorn note in the determinedly optimistic ending to an ensuing letter to him: 'I'm afraid my recent letters have vacillated between the frantic and the tedious. I'm sorry, I was, and still am, very emotionally exhausted. [...] The springs of delights will flow again no doubt' (26 September 1946). But a year later, even on the night before she left Chiswick for Cambridge, it was still a struggle not to succumb. She told Queneau, 'I can't decide whether or not I'm very depressed this evening. I suppose I'd better decide not to be' (5 October 1947). Cambridge did lift her mood to the point where she could admit to him, 'Since you ask, yes I suppose I am (almost) happy. The first time in years. I love my work and I like the community I belong to' (6 November 1947), but this was after much difficulty in settling in there, and is still qualified, 'almost'. In Oxford the following year, things are no better for her. In the spring, 'Life has been saddening and complex, as usual, tho' more so' (31 May 1950); in the summer, 'I'm very depressed at present. [...] I'll write properly when I feel saner. You know how one's thoughts can be a pack of wolves' (6 June 1950), and again, 'I'm very depressed at present. It will be good to be in Paris – I suppose this can't fail to cheer me up, tho' I can't at the moment imagine how anything would' (4 August 1950); and in the autumn, 'the stoical superscription [in two books Queneau had sent her] fits my present mood, which is a disposition to practise gritting the teeth in the face of almost inevitable failure' (25 October 1950). Nor do things change a year on when she tells Lidderdale, 'There is a midsummer melancholy upon me' (29 June 1951).

As the next chapter will reveal, there were multiple causes for Iris Murdoch's low and troubled spirits. During her 'Nadir' year in Chiswick she suffered greatly from loneliness, telling Queneau, 'MacKinnon at Oxford seems to be going through some sort of spiritual crisis & can't see me. A bunch of goddamn neurotics I have for friends' (14 July 1946) and 'I know many pleasant people in London, most of whom are a bit queer & emotionally unstable. (Those on whom I was proposing to depend seem to be proposing to depend on me.)' (22 July 1946). People are all important to her. She writes to Queneau, 'In my own difficulties I found that the love of certain people supported me more than almost anything else' (6 December 1946) and 'I don't care a hang this evening about anything theoretical. I care so much more about people, indeed I always do. I am so grateful, when I think about it, to the people I love for being so loveable (5

October 1947). She longs for his companionship and for the atmosphere of France that year:

> I'd like to talk with you – this afternoon, say – enormously at leisure, sitting outside some café in the Boulevard something-or-other, with the sparrows hopping on the table and the people passing and discuss universal History and Human Destiny and our history and our destiny, and politics and language – I need so much to talk and talk – but the chances to rarely come. (24 April 1947)

But even when she caught up with old friends and met new ones at Cambridge and Oxford, Iris Murdoch's relationships brought her more pain than pleasure at this stage in her life. Thus she tells Queneau the following year, 'I'm very moody at present, and in an emotional tangle which will have God knows what outcome' (17 February 1952). Such entanglements were not the sole cause of her despondency – her writing was also a source of anguish at this time – but they were a large measure of the reason for her unhappiness in her late twenties and early thirties, as the next chapter will investigate.

Chapter Two

The Flesh: Sex, Marriage and John Bayley

It is a truth universally acknowledged, that a single woman in possession of no fortune must be in want of a husband.

(with apologies to Jane Austen)

I feel sorry for the lonely depressed young woman we left in the last chapter, but it has to be said, much of Iris Murdoch's trouble was of her own making – as is the case with her fictional characters. That assertion needs qualifying with the acknowledgement that history again plays a huge part in human affairs. A major element in biographical writing is seeing how the desires and drives of individual subjects intersect with the ruthless thrust of their historical circumstances over which they have no control – the contingency which Iris Murdoch discusses in her philosophy and depicts in her novels.

In 1939, whilst still an undergraduate, Iris Murdoch declared, 'I *long* to get married, I'd do *anything* to get married' (*IMAL*, 95). A normal desire, if extravagantly expressed. But it was to be a long hard road for her towards this goal. Had it not been for the Second World War, Frank Thompson would not have been shot in Bulgaria in June 1944. Iris Murdoch was his 'dream-girl – a poetic Irish Communist' (*WW*, 82) and he was her fellow Communist and very close friend at Oxford. They had a deep epistolary relationship during the war and without him she was not only bereaved but lonely for letters.[27] Movingly, Iris Murdoch was given a volume of Catullus and a Byzantine coin which he had with him on his death. But she had lost him. Later she was to lose another beloved man, Franz Baermann Steiner, whose family died in concentration camps. Iris Murdoch felt he too was 'one of Hitler's victims' (*IMAL*, 322). The gravity of these bereavements cannot be underestimated.

Iris Murdoch's attitude to sexual relationships was unconventional, to say the least. On 12 December 1948, she wrote in her journal: 'One of my more fundamental assumptions is that I have the power to seduce anyone' (*IMAL*, 283). By this point in her life she had already proved her claim, and – as in chapter one – a brief note on 'Previously in my life ...' will indicate the range and complexity of her conquests. Frank Thompson, Noel Martin, Leo Pliatzky, David Hicks and Patrick O'Regan were among those who fell in love with her at Oxford, where she herself was infatuated with two older married men, her tutors Donald MacKinnon and Eduard Fraenkel, the latter notorious for pawing female students. (This may have laid the ground for Iris Murdoch's obsession with the erotic element in teacher-pupil relationships which surfaces in her novels.) In London, she lost her virginity though she never names the man. She shared 'Seaforth', her London eyrie, with Philippa Bosanquet, her friend from Oxford and fellow philosopher. While living there Iris Murdoch was simultaneously involved with Thomas Balogh, an 'emotional fascist' (*IMAL*, 185) and previous lover of Philippa's, and with Michael (M.R.D.) Foot, whom she hurt deeply and whom Philippa later married. Unsurprisingly this caused much tension.

Iris Murdoch's seductive power, which cannot be denied, is something of a mystery. Conradi acknowledges that 'she was not conventionally pretty' and cites Frank Thompson saying that her figure was 'too thick to be good' (*WW*, 90). John Bayley recalls a comment that she was 'like a little bull' (Bayley, 14). Yet Iris Murdoch boasted of her pulling power in her journal. Bayley also remembers 'how diabolically attractive everyone else found her' (Bayley, 19), and Conradi's admission that even before 1945 'the number of her devotees is at first sight uncomfortable' (*WW*, 90) comes to seem an understatement in the light of her sexual behaviour over the following decade.

Characters in Iris Murdoch's novels are woven into webs of desire so complex as to be farcical. People love more than one person at the same time; they love bisexually, adulterously, incestuously. She has been criticized for this but she would strenuously deny that it is untrue to life. It was certainly not untrue to her own life. As Conradi recounts:

[...] she was furious when told that Aristotle had argued that one could be in love with only one person at a time: her own experience told her that Aristotle must be wrong. That her approach to love appeared strange to some never bothered her. She accordingly ran close friendships and love-affairs concurrently. (*WW*, 91)

A quick survey of her emotional entanglements between 1945 and 1956 reads more dramatically than any of her own convoluted love plots.

The men in Iris Murdoch's life...

In November 1945 she becomes engaged to David Hicks but soon admits to him that she slept with a French lorry driver after a drunken party, also with a Parisian boy (*WW*, 285, 297). Hicks breaks off the engagement in February 1946 finding Iris Murdoch too 'formidable' (*WW*, 303). Just two days later she meets Raymond Queneau after whom she pines for many years to come. Back in England in 1947, she picks up with Donald MacKinnon – whom she had previously ceased to see because of his wife's discomfort: her relationship with him, though chaste, is intense. She claims to have sexual adventures (including homosexual ones) during a trip to Paris (where she also sees Queneau).

Her year in Cambridge seems without sexual complications, but once she gets back to Oxford the pace quickens. From January to November 1949 she has a brief but intense involvement with Fred Broadie and in February 1950 falls in love with an English Fellow at Lincoln College, Wallace Robson. That relationship, which leads to a semi-engagement, ends in April 1952. But during this time she also has a short passionate love affair with a political philosopher at Nuffield College, Michael Oakeshott, from October to December 1950. This ends when he, like Hicks, falls in love with another woman and Iris Murdoch is again very hurt – though not bothered about how she is hurting Robson at this time. In May 1951 she meets Franz Steiner, to whom she draws increasingly close, but in 1952 she is also becoming close to the Professor of Ancient History at University College London, the married Jewish-Italian Arnold Momigliano. On Sunday 1 June 1952 she spends time with both men, one after the other, and then on the 29 June passionately kisses Ferrucio Rossi-Landi, an Italian semiotician, whilst an historian from Worcester College, Asa Briggs, also falls in love with her. In August she and Momigliano become lovers while travelling in Italy, and later that same month she writes a passionate fourteen-page letter declaring her love to Queneau. (It is not reciprocated.) In October she is attracted to Maurice Charlton, a medical student at Hertford College, but continues the deepening relationship with Steiner which ends abruptly and shockingly with his premature death (aged forty-three) on 27 November – in bed with Iris Murdoch according to the (unverifiable) account of his friend, the Nobel Prize winning Bulgarian author, Elias Canetti.

At Steiner's funeral the following day, Iris Murdoch encounters Canetti. It is to him she turns in her grief – though Robson and Momigliano profess continuing love for her – and in January 1953 she begins a three-year love affair with Canetti to whom she becomes enthralled. (It is no coincidence that it is at this point that her second published novel, *The Flight from the Enchanter*, begins to germinate in Iris Murdoch's mind.) In August 1953 she travels to Italy with Momigliano again, and in the autumn meets John Bayley – who has already noticed her bicycling past his study window – at a cocktail party at St Anne's. On 5 February 1954 Iris Murdoch confesses to her journal that she is becoming fond of her new admirer, they see each other increasingly frequently, and on 14 June she notes in her journal that she determines not to harm or hurt him, though – telling him about Momigliano, Briggs and Canetti – she admits that she can only offer him 'a *sort* of constancy' (Purton, 67). And indeed, after she falls in love with John Bayley on 3 June, Iris Murdoch astonishingly accepts Canetti's decree that she must not have sexual relations with this man; when they visit Paris in July she insists that she and John Bayley stay at separate hotels, though by September she rejects the decree. Meanwhile, in August she travels to France and Italy with a Jewish-Greek philosopher, John Simopoulos (though they were not lovers), and the following August 1955 she goes to Italy with Momigliano again.

... and the women

And that resumé only covers the *men* in her life during this period. John Bayley denies that Iris Murdoch ever had lesbian relationships, and conceals the reason for her leaving St Anne's – ostensibly to dedicate her time to writing instead of teaching (though she immediately went to teach at the Royal College of Art) – but actually to prevent a scandal at the college. However, Iris Murdoch has an intense though not physical relationship with Elizabeth Anscombe, her fellow philosopher, in December 1950, and in June 1952 she passionately kisses Peter Ady, a female Economics tutor at St Anne's which leads to a quiet affair. The two women go to France together in September 1955; that autumn Iris Murdoch also begins an intense relationship with the novelist Brigid Brophy which fades out by February 1956 and in April 1956 she goes to France with Peter Ady again (Purton, 52, 60, 71-3). Light may be shed on Iris Murdoch's behaviour with other women by a comment she made in a letter to Queneau with regard to Simone de Beauvoir's seminal book *Le Deuxième Sexe* which she read immediately after it was first published in June 1949:

> I don't know <u>what</u> I think of this work, except that it interests & pleases me. (I find that, selon Miss de Beauvoir, in various respects in which I thought I was abnormal I appear to be normal!) (How remarkably little these matters are talked of. It's striking –). (4 December 1949)

The fourth chapter of part one of *Le Deuxième Sexe*, 'La lesbienne', is a description of sexual relations with women which de Beauvoir believed that society considers a 'forbidden path'. There is no proof that this is what Iris

Murdoch had in mind by the elusive term 'these matters'; the use of parenthesis and elliptical ending suggest that although she finds it striking that 'these matters' are little talked of, she does not feel able to do so overtly herself. Bravely writing of male homosexuality (before it was decriminalized in England) in her fourth novel, *The Bell*, Murdoch never really explores female homosexuality in her fiction. What this silence portends is a matter for conjecture. But in her own life she appears to have embraced all available sexual experience. This did not necessarily make for happiness. Indeed she wrote to Queneau, 'No, I'm not in love, thank God. Amoureuse/ heureuse are contradictories in my universe of discourse' (6 November 1947), and later, that I 'have been on the rack over various personal problems – still not resolved' (10 May 1950). But she was no less desperate to get married and she knew the effect this was having on her. She told Queneau that she was 'bothered about trying to marry somebody but it didn't come off. Just as well maybe' and adds with painful self-awareness, 'If I could only stop thinking about marriage maybe I'd get some work done' (13 March 1951). The following year, the parenthetical note sounds bitterly wistful when she tells him, 'I'll write decently when the present chaos of final exams, garden parties, sherry parties, weddings (not mine) are over' (27 May 1952). By now her philosopher friends from undergraduate days were all married: Elizabeth Anscombe in 1941; Philippa Bosanquet in 1945; Mary Scrutton in 1950, and – rubbing salt into the wound – Iris Murdoch was asked to be her bridesmaid.

Ten days that positively shook the world

Iris Murdoch, never one to fear to tread where fools rush in, *se lança même dans* (launched herself into) love affairs just as she did with reading, writing, translating, indeed *living*. After Frank Thompson's death and before she went abroad Iris Murdoch wrote to David Hicks: 'Sometimes though I feel desperate again for human intimacy & a man & the insanities of being in love' (*WW*, 223). Desperation and insanity are key notes that sound more loudly as she moves into her thirties and fears never marrying, despite her ambivalence about the married state. Hicks himself was her next hope after Frank's untimely death, and in her letters to him she writes of wanting to bear his children and of 'bringing them up beautifully' in 'a house in Bucks' (*WW*, 259, 269). Had that transpired, would we have had the novels? (One wonders the same thing about Jane Austen and Virginia Woolf, also childless.) Obviously these were dreams of a fantasy future but they give the lie to John Bayley's claim that 'Iris's attitude towards procreation, as to sex, was not dismissive: it was detachedly and benevolently indifferent. She herself had other things to do' (Bayley, 69). That may have become true by that point in her life, but at this earlier stage she was keeping her options open.

Hicks was not to be the one that she married, however.[28] She describes what happened as *une histoire de fous* in a letter to Lidderdale:

> I went home on leave in November [...] in order to see David Hicks. It was a tornado. Ten days that

positively shook the world. I suppose I had expected something, but not a great soul-rendering drama such as we actually met. On the second day we decided that we would get married. [....] about 10 days ago I get a long lyrical letter saying that he has met [...] a WONDERFUL girl [...] and that he is very much in love with her, and suggesting in a final line or two that maybe we'd better call our arrangements off. I wrote back at once, saying yes, call them off [...] After the initial shock, my main feeling is extreme relief, and amazement at the period of temporary insanity. [...] It was an odd business altogether. A very narrow escape. [...] Now the spell is completely and finally broken & I feel thoroughly happy and integrated and free, only with an increased horror of all ties, especially marital. [...] I hope I shall not again give vein to this dangerous faculty for choosing the second rate. (28 February 1946)

This brisk resumé conceals the pain evident in her letters to Hicks himself and shows her trying to grow a carapace against hurt.

A tissue of foolishnesses

The pain of such rejection was bad: the pain of loss through death worse. After Steiner's death Iris Murdoch wrote sombrely to Queneau:

Things are not very well. Someone whom I loved very deeply and from whom I was beginning to hope very much has died suddenly. Everything is changed. Strange, how all wishes & interests can perish, I measure now how much tied to this one person. I regret wasted time. At the moment I can't see how to get on at all. [...] One knew this might happen – but didn't expect it, or I didn't. I couldn't believe in the possibility of death. I wrote you a foolish letter in the summer – tho' it was 'sincere'. My whole existence seems to me now such a tissue of foolishnesses. My feelings where you are concerned are necessarily, through force of circumstance, 'abstract'. But this man who has died was daily bread. I knew this, of course, even at the time. (13 December 1952)

Losing Franz as well as Frank was a brutal double blow. In such a low state Iris Murdoch was easy prey for Canetti (as were many others) and it took her a long time to escape from his thrall, or even to want to.

How much are biographers allowed to speculate? My reading between the lines of her life suggests to me that one of Iris Murdoch's fantasies was of being a *hetæra*, a Great Mistress (courtesans feature in her novels, and she was fascinated by *The Tale of Genji*) and that she would have liked to play de Beauvoir to a Sartre of her own, could she have found one, (Queneau for preference). But her experience with this mode of living in relation to Canetti did not, she found, make for happiness. Nor – importantly – did it make space for her to write. And nor – as the next three chapters will show – did it encompass the entirety of her being. Sex matters, but other things ultimately matter more, and when the burning question of whom she should marry was sorted she was able to put sex at a greater distance and write.

Some day my prince will come

Conradi nicely describes John Bayley as 'an improbable rescuer' (*IMAL*, 374) but his patience and persistence beat the 'Hampstead Monster' as he calls Canetti (Bayley, 117). It is significant that Iris Murdoch referred often in her journal to John Bayley's laughter and noted his beaming smile when he met her at a London station (Purton, 67-8). She, naturally quite solemn, needed that life-giving quality. With him she could be another self, a self she had either lost or had never discovered; a child-like self. They danced wildly and prattled like children together (Purton, 67). He did not find her formidable, just loveable. He was exactly what she needed. And he could cope with her past – though his memoirs indicate how costly that was for him.

John Bayley's memories of Iris Murdoch are in no way gospel truth, as he himself acknowledges. He is shaping the past in ways that are acceptable to his own psyche (as well as artfully turning them into a patterned narrative pleasing to the reader). He tells us that:

Iris had several lovers, often apparently at the same time [...] she usually gave her favours out of admiration and respect: for, so to speak, the godlike rather than the conventionally attractive or sexual attributes in the men who pursued her. Men who were like gods for her were also for her erotic beings, but sex was something she regarded as rather marginal, not an end in itself. (Bayley, 46)

This strikes me both as half-true and as self-protective. Sex is certainly not marginal in Iris Murdoch's fiction, nor does it appear so in her life up to this point. In her novels sex is a source of humour as in Restoration Comedy and Bedroom Farce. It is also, along with all human activities, put into a ludicrous light by the hilarious tirades of the dying elderly father figure in *A Fairly Honourable Defeat*:

'What a rubbishy arrangement sex is,' said Leonard Browne. 'And I don't just mean the machinery of it, though that's stupid enough in all conscience. A projection upon one body is laboriously inserted into a hole in another. It's the invention of a mere mechanic and a very fumbling and unimaginative one at that. I remember when someone told me about it at school I simply didn't believe him. I thought it couldn't turn out to be something so grotesque. Later on when I had more of a stake in it I persuaded myself otherwise. But now that's all past and done with I can see it again for what it is, a pitiful awkward ugly inefficient piece of fleshy mechanism.'[29]

But Iris Murdoch's novels also portray the dark side of sex as a means of power over others, which she had personally experienced. However John Bayley helped her escape from this darker side through 'common sense' and marriage:

> Falling in love with people who represented for her
> spiritual authority, wisdom, beneficence, even a force
> that might seem darkly ambiguous and enigmatic,
> was an adventure in the soul's progress and
> experience; she craved it, needed it, but she was far
> too sensible ever to become enslaved [...] she could
> get away when she wanted: common sense was the
> final arbiter of her emotional impulses. (Bayley, 66)

In the end she did flee the enchanter. And she exploited
that experience, as all others, through her work.

Iris Murdoch's relationship with her husband was
utterly different. In his own words once again (I think
he *deserves* a voice in someone else's impertinent account
of his own marriage and also merits it as he expresses
things so perfectly and with such touching humility),
John Bayley accounts for her choosing him as a life
partner thus:

> She seemed to be giving way to some deep need of
> which she had been wholly unconscious: the need to
> throw away not only the manoeuvres and rivalries
> of intellect, but the emotional fears and fascinations,
> the power struggles and surrenders of adult loving.
> (Bayley, 30)

Iris Murdoch's parents' marriage was, so John Bayley
thinks, a *mariage blanc* (*IMAL*, 49) – with who knows what
subliminal effect on their daughter's own sexuality – and
her own marriage was centred more in companionship
than in passion. The image of a happy marriage in her

novels is often of two good animals living quietly in a hutch together. Her fiction gives the dominant impression that passion occurs outside connubial relationships, as for her it seems to have done. Moreover, John Bayley felt how reluctant Iris Murdoch was to commit herself. Curiously, it seems to have been Elizabeth Bowen's influence that overcame Iris Murdoch's fears. In July 1956 Iris Murdoch was invited to stay at Bowen's Court in County Cork. This visit would have fed enormously into her own romanticized sense of Irishness, and the attention of Elizabeth Bowen, senior to Iris Murdoch, superior to her in the subtle miasma of Irish social stratification, and an admired established novelist, must have been deeply flattering. She told her guest how vital her own husband, Alan Cameron, was to her, and presented her with a vision of a marriage within which a woman could be freed to write, rather than prevented. Intriguing from this biographer's point of view is John Bayleys' aside that the two women had 'insensibly [...] got onto the question of *how one decided things in life*' (Bayley, 95, my italics), a question that enters Iris Murdoch's philosophy but here had direct personal application – how do you decide whether and whom to marry? Whatever the cause, Iris Murdoch suddenly married John Bayley on 14 August 1956, the month after she returned from her visit to Elizabeth Bowen. The wedding was very low key and Iris Murdoch noted in the margin of her journal – as if to keep the marriage off the centre of her inner stage – 'August 14. Married John.'

The marriage, however, worked well for both partners for almost forty years, ending only when Iris's death did them part. Neither seems quite to have believed in it. John Bayley describes them as 'naughty children together', and sees them appearing to others as 'two such absurd if engaging creatures [...] pretending to be husband and wife', 'two quaint children rather than a married couple.' (Bayley, 13, 141). Vitally, John Bayley accorded his wife's work prime importance and created freedom for her to write. Thus he cooked, because 'the point was that Iris was working – properly working – and I was determined that she should not be distracted from this.' (Bayley, 102). Ironically, this domestic scenario harks back to Iris Murdoch's engagement to David Hicks at the start of this chapter. In a letter to Hicks on 19 January 1946, she admits:

> I find it difficult to see how exactly it will take me, this business of being a wife. Whether I shall really get interested in cooking and tidying the house & so on, or whether I shall have a bright snappy job of some kind & drag you out to restaurants to eat [...] or whether I shall selfishly bury myself in books, dreamily emerging when you return home to make you some ghastly undercooked meal. Darling, what risks you're running! (*WW*, 284)

He broke it off. But over ten years later, older, much sadder and perhaps wiser, Iris Murdoch found a man who was prepared to run the risk. Marrying John Bayley was the start of a new life for her.

Chapter Three

The Spirit: Theology, Spirituality and Simone Weil

Not that I have 'finished with religion'. I haven't begun yet.

Iris Murdoch

E mphasis on Iris Murdoch the (bi)sexual being, indeed the 'loose woman', necessarily distorts the picture of her as a whole. This chapter will look at Iris Murdoch the spiritual being, and give so different an impression of her that one might be forgiven for wondering if this can possibly be the same person. The myth of Proteas – a Greek sea-god who could change his shape to appear as different animals or even elements (fire, water) – was deeply important to Iris Murdoch, as she herself was such a shape-shifter. I want to repeat the desiderata for her life that she outlined to Queneau which I quoted in chapter one:

> I think nothing is really worth anything except (a) being happily married, (b) being a saint, (c) writing a good novel. My chances of (a) diminish yearly, (b) is far too difficult – there remains (c) which still inspires hope. (16 March 1950)

So far in this biography, she has achieved (a) despite what she saw as her diminishing chances. Notwithstanding her sexual adventures, Iris Murdoch had not given up on (b) either, despite the daunting nature of the aspiration. I want now to trace the trajectory of her spiritual journey during this fraught period of her development.

But first we need again to look at 'Previously in my life …' with regard to Iris Murdoch's religious education. John Bayley, who confesses to having 'very little understanding of the spiritual life' himself (Bayley, 38), makes oddly contradictory claims, saying at one point that 'Iris's childhood was happily godless' (Bayley, 66), then at another declaring of Iris Murdoch and her parents: 'None of the three had religion: all were, in the theological sense, naturally Christian souls' (Bayley, 170). This does not accord with Iris Murdoch's sense of herself as not only Irish, but an Irish *Protestant*, with her memories of her mother Rene teaching her prayers and religious songs ('Tell me the old, old story of Jesus and His love') as a child (*IMAL*, 31), or with her consistent statements in interview: to Jack Biles in 1977, 'I am not myself a Christian believer, but I was brought up as a Christian and I feel close to Christianity'; to John Haffenden in 1983, 'I can't get away from the Christ who travels with me; I was Christian as a child'; and to Jonathan Miller in 1988, 'my mother was an Anglican, my father a Quaker, a sort of Quaker. And they assumed that I would learn Christianity, and be religious and pray, and I think I could pray as soon as I could speak. And I knew that God was present' (Dooley, 62, 136, 209). Badminton, though a liberal and free-thinking school had as its motto, *'Pro omnibus quisque, pro Deo omnes'* – 'Each for all, all for God' – and BMB, the head, was sympathetic to Quaker ideals. There were Morning Assemblies and Evening Prayers and pupils were required to attend a church on Sundays. Iris Murdoch seems to have gone to a mixture of Congregational and Anglican services, and visited Quaker Meetings too. In her teens she was confirmed as a member of the Anglican Church, so a fairly firm religious start in life.

However, that does not mean that John Bayley is wide of the mark when he says that 'her appetite for the spiritual developed in her Oxford days, nurtured by Plato and by her studies in philosophy. It was part of the inner world of her imagination and never appeared on the surface' (Bayley, 66). For Iris Murdoch, religion and philosophy are not in opposition but intertwined and concerned with the same basic issues. I have ordered these chapters with deliberation because at this stage of her life she seems to move from theology towards philosophy – towards 'Good' from 'God' – and then to move again towards art, as novel-writing became her chief (though not her only) occupation. It is never possible to make clear-cut distinctions where Iris Murdoch is concerned. For her, life was very much all of a piece, with sex and religion and philosophy and art flashing different lights from the prism of human experience. It is simply that she was forced to choose the main endeavour into which she would pour most of her time and energy – though it greatly frustrated her to have her scope thus limited.

Letters to Queneau after Iris Murdoch's return to England trace her path first towards and then away from institutional Christianity – to be firmly distinguished from the figure of Christ, which remained iconic to her. Back home in Chiswick, during that awful autumn of 1946, she tells him:

As an act of the combat with my disarray I recently spent a week with an enclosed community of Benedictine nuns in Kent. This was a remarkable experience. Discipline and control of that kind – i.e. when united with a spontaneous love and tenderness (such certainty – I have forgotten what it means to be certain, when I see that word 'love'.) – can be very healing and strengthening. I often wish I could be Christian. There is such worth there – & values which are <u>real</u> to one – but the rest remains a fairy tale to me.

Also much picturesque detail (of course!) Van Eyckish light on white wimples and jewelled crosses, the beautiful unwearying plainsong, speaking though a grille […] Life is very strange isn't it? (15, October 1946)

At Cambridge the following year she confides in him:

> Much political and religious tension (in me I
> mean) at the moment. A feeling of dishonesty &
> divided loyalties. I expect I shall have to become a
> Christian sooner or later. All my thought drives in
> that direction. Ecclesia Anglicana tho', not Romana.
> Another compromise. (6 November 1947)

Distaste for ecclesiastical hierarchy (which her novels
gleefully mock) is glimpsed in a rueful remark: 'Was
immersed [...] in a Christian conference (oh dear,
bishops)' (15 September 1949). Some years later she
tells Queneau, 'I have by now in effect drifted out of
the Christian church. This matter causes me distress.
But there it is. Not that I have "finished with religion".
I haven't begun yet' (11 January 1953). The established
Church was not the place in which Iris Murdoch found
it possible to explore her own religious thoughts and
experiences. But it was not for want of trying over this
crucial decade.

During that time Iris Murdoch was influenced by many
people, some of them atheists as Sartre, Queneau, Canetti
(and indeed John Bayley) all were. Others, however, were
passionately religious. Donald Mackinnon for one – she
saw him as a Christ figure (with herself in the role of
Mary Magdalene – as I am emphasizing throughout, sex
and religion did not live in separate compartments in Iris
Murdoch's head). Another was her friend from Oxford,
Lucy Klatschko, who, after being a wild undergraduate,
was received into the Roman Catholic Church in

1952, became a postulant at Stanbrook Abbey near Worcester on 1 May 1954, and spent the rest of her life as Sister Marian, with whom Iris Murdoch maintained correspondence and visited.[30] Iris Murdoch tasted the religious life herself, going three times to Malling Abbey in Kent; in October 1946 (the visit about which she wrote to Queneau in the letter above), in August 1948, and again in August 1949, when she made a Retreat under the spiritual direction of Canon Dart. In London she attended services at Westminster Cathedral and in Cambridge she sought out the Chaplain of the Anglican Franciscan House, Father Denis Marsh – though she felt disloyal to the Communist Party for doing so.

All through these years Iris Murdoch was voraciously reading theology as well as philosophy and literature. She read Augustine, whose treatise *The City of God* was given to her in March 1947 by BMB, her old headmistress, who continued to be an influence in her life. (John Bayley was taken to visit BMB for her approval). She read *Moses* by Martin Buber which Donald Mackinnon gave her in July 1947. In November that year she was studying Julian of Norwich alongside Wittgenstein, again relating spirituality and philosophy and puzzling over their interconnections.

One of the many paths not taken by Iris Murdoch, but another discipline in which she would have had a distinctive voice, is theology. She was dissatisfied with the divorce of theology from philosophy which prevailed in both the French and British philosophical climate in the early to mid-twentieth century, because her questioning of life embraced spiritual as well as purely intellectual matters. In this she was not alone. In October 1948, when she had just returned to Oxford to teach at St Anne's College, a small group of like-minded people started an informal discussion group called the 'Metaphysicals' and Iris Murdoch, a 'wistful seeker' (*IMAL*, 305), was at the inaugural meeting in Christ Church. She was the only woman: the others were male High Anglicans. (Iris Murdoch is often the sole female in various groups: after her fictional début with *Under the Net* she was included – briefly and erroneously – with the 1950s novelists dubbed the 'Angry Young Men'; one of her early essays, 'A House of Theory' was written for a book called *Conviction* which is described on the dust cover as a collection of essays by a dozen 'Thoughtful Young Men';[31] and in maturity, she is the only woman philosopher in Bryan Magee's book entitled *Men of Ideas*.[32] It is noteworthy that every one of the first-person narrators in her novels is male; she never wrote from a female perspective. Perhaps these experiences made it feel 'normal' to her to think and write 'as a man'.) The purpose of the 'Metaphysicals' was to bring religious metaphysics and theological discourse back into the arena of discussion from which it had been ejected by the anti-metaphysical bias of the linguistically orientated analytic philosophy which was then dominant. Iris Murdoch gave a paper to the group on 25 October 1950 and continued to meet with them until 1953 when she left, feeling that her path had diverged from theirs. But she continued to believe it important for religious thinking and experience to be included in philosophical discussion and she praised the Socratic Club (a group begun in 1941 to which she gave a paper early in 1952) for having the courage to promote dialogue between philosophy and theology and to allow discussion of issues outlawed by the prevailing intellectual mood of the time.

Iris Murdoch herself engaged in discussion with strong Christian believers at different points of the spectrum, from Roman Catholic nuns to Evangelical Anglicans. She was *interested* in religion. But, as her philosophy would later argue and her novels demonstrate, she was ultimately unable to accept the grand narrative of Christianity which has shaped human thought (and art) in the western world for good and ill. The stance that she was to maintain was developed as she read and talked during these years – a stance which can roughly be described thus. Iris Murdoch rejects the concepts of a personal God and of eternal life. Furthermore, she quarrels with the central metaphysical hermeneutic of Christianity – its pivotal focus on the suffering and death of Christ as a means of atonement and redemption – because she finds this meta-narrative not only intellectually untenable, but morally objectionable. It goes against the grain of her understanding of the nature of Good. One must be good for nothing, not for the personal gain she sees as involved in this 'payback' of being pardoned and offered salvation.

The only genuine way to be good is to be good 'for nothing'

John Bayley self-deprecatingly says 'Iris is good. I'm not good inside, but I can get by on being nice' (Bayley, 171), and gives it as his opinion that 'Iris was both a nice child and a good one, and her parents were the same'

(Bayley, 170). In her novel *The Nice and the Good*, Iris Murdoch, subtly and amusingly but also importantly, differentiates between the two concepts. Theo Gray, a spiritually damaged character, 'had begun to glimpse the distance which separates the nice from the good, and the vision of this gap had terrified his soul' (348) and he thinks:

> The point is that nothing matters except loving what is good. Not to look at evil but to look at good. Only this contemplation breaks the tyranny of the past, breaks the adherence of evil to the personality, breaks, in the end, the personality itself. (344)

In her philosophy, Iris Murdoch makes the same point. She is impatient with the impoverishment of contemporary philosophy and fiction saying that 'if a moral philosophy does not give a satisfactory or sufficiently rich account of what we unphilosophically know to be goodness, then away with it' (*Existentialists and Mystics*, 205). She asks what a good man is like (*EM*, 342) and tries to depict good people in her novels – a difficult task as evil people are notoriously more interesting, and the truly good become strangely invisible. She wants to restore dignity and authority to the concept of Good (*EM*, 333) and her central beliefs are that:

> The Good has nothing to do with purpose, indeed it excludes the idea of purpose. 'All is vanity' is the beginning and the end of ethics. The only genuine way to be good is to be good 'for nothing' in the midst

of a scene where every 'natural' thing, including one's own mind is subject to chance, that is, to necessity. (*EM*, 358)

For Iris Murdoch 'it is the fundamental task of each person to make himself good' (*MGM*, 362). Put at its strongest, one of the only things 'worth anything' is 'being a saint', but that, as she acknowledges, is very difficult. That did not stop her from trying: she was as persistent in her striving towards saintliness as she was in her striving to get married and to get a novel published. The search for the Good and how to *become* good is something that increasingly occupied Iris Murdoch's mind and in the lived context of her own particular existence – the only arena in which anyone can seek to become good or saintly – this posed considerable challenges.

Despite John Bayley's opinion, Iris Murdoch was no more naturally good than anyone else (one has to allow for the rose-coloured spectacles worn by an uxorious husband). On the contrary, she was fiercely ambitious, and greedy for success, attention and love. Her self-centred behaviour hurt many people including those of whom she was fond, like Michael and Philippa Foot, as we saw in the last chapter. It is not surprising that she told Queneau 'I regret many things' (15 September 1946). But regret is the beginning of self-awareness and can lead to repentance (which can be a secular as well as a religious experience – a subtle concept which Iris Murdoch's later fiction will repeatedly explore) and to deep change in one's life.

Simone Weil said that morality was a matter of attention, not of will. We need a new vocabulary of attention [33]

The greatest help that Iris Murdoch received with this arduous spiritual endeavour came through the writings of the Jewish-French philosopher and mystic Simone Weil. Weil is another of the most significant figures in Iris Murdoch's development, both as a philosopher and novelist, and in her own personal spiritual quest. She only wrote about Weil's work directly once, in 'Knowing the Void' a short review of *The Notebooks of Simone Weil* published in November 1956, the same year that she got married – and the final year in the parameters of this study of how she became Iris Murdoch. Weil was an intrinsic and crucial part of that process. (That single review is augmented by the notable fact that Weil is the only female philosopher whose work is discussed in *Metaphysics as a Guide to Morals*.) Iris Murdoch was making a deep study of Weil's idiosyncratic and mystical philosophy during these formative years. She owned nineteen books by Weil which she filled with annotations and marginalia, though sadly she did not date them so it is hard to tell exactly when she read each one.[34] (She taught Weil's text *Attente de Dieu* to her undergraduate students with a fine disregard for the Oxford syllabus.) Weil's personality and ascetic life exercised Murdoch's imagination and this is reflected in her novels, particularly in the character of Anne Cavidge in *Nuns and Soldiers*. But it is the concept of *attention* which Iris Murdoch borrowed from Weil and developed as her own. This is both a philosophical and spiritual concept and it is central to the process of change which Murdoch describes by the rather awkward but expressive word *unselfing*, a discipline of expelling (or at least diminishing) the clamour of what she calls the 'fat relentless ego' which, in her view, is the enemy of the moral life (*EM*, 342).

This all sounds horribly difficult and arcane. But it is in fact very simple to understand – though anything but simple to practise. Iris Murdoch put it very visually and memorably in a passage in her treatise *The Sovereignty of Good* – a book which contains the kernel of her message:

> I am looking out of my window in an anxious and resentful state of mind, oblivious of my own surroundings, brooding perhaps on some damage done to my prestige. Then suddenly I observe a hovering kestrel. In a moment everything is altered. The brooding self with its hurt vanity has disappeared. There is nothing now but kestrel. And when I return to thinking of the other matter it seems less important. And of course this is something which we may also do deliberately: give attention to nature in order to clear our minds of selfish care. (*EM*, 369)

This vivid description makes it clear that Iris Murdoch experienced the painful human states of anxiety and resentment, hurt vanity and selfish care. But she learnt how to overcome them through this technique of attention and she strove by this means to progress in 'unselfing'. For her, the convent and the church were not the place for growth in holiness, and traditional prayer was not the means. She found secular equivalents for these sacred spaces and secular channels of grace.

Art galleries and paintings serve the purpose as well as the natural world. This is best explained by a scene in *The Bell* which shows attention to art having moral effect upon a character, Dora Greenfield, who is distressed and confused by her unhappy marriage and her lack of direction in life. She goes into the National Gallery in London and aimlessly wanders around looking at the paintings until her attention is arrested by one in particular:

> Dora stopped at last in front of Gainsborough's picture of his two daughters. These children step through a wood hand in hand, their garments shimmering, their eyes serious and dark, their two pale heads, round full buds, like yet unlike.
> Dora was always moved by the pictures. Today she was moved, but in a new way. She marvelled, with a kind of gratitude, that they were all still here, and her heart was filled with love for the pictures, their authority, their marvellous generosity, their splendour. It occurred to her that here at last was something real and something perfect. [...] Here was something which her consciousness could not wretchedly devour, and by making it part of her fantasy make it worthless. [...] the pictures were something real outside herself, which spoke to her kindly and yet in sovereign tones, something superior and good whose presence destroyed the dreary trance-like solipsism of her earlier mood. (190-1)

Iris Murdoch could write of these experiences of kestrels and paintings because she had had them herself and profited by them. She transfigured them into art in her novels which thus act as a conduit of her spiritual learning to her readers. But she also transformed herself through them, changing from a self-centred young woman who damaged those around her and felt remorse for doing so, to a spiritually mature mentor and guide to many readers.

John Bayley describes Iris Murdoch as being humble. In this instance I think he is accurate rather than blindly adoring. But I think she was *becoming* humble and by the time she met him she had travelled some distance on her difficult journey towards saintliness. She describes the 'good man' as having humility and says: 'Only rarely does one meet somebody in whom it positively shines, in whom one apprehends with amazement the absence of the anxious avaricious tentacles of the self' (*EM*, 385). She was busy on the invisible spiritual work – a kind of inward change of which she insists philosophy must take account – of stripping her own ego of those anxious avaricious tentacles. Her success in so doing is testified to not only by her husband who describes 'a natural goodness in her' as 'something angelic' and says 'she seems herself the presence found in an icon' (Bayley, 59), but also by those who met her later in her life who did find her such a holy presence and who felt there was something saintly about her. There was. But it was nothing esoteric. It was the quality – so rare as to be remarkable – of giving the other her full attention, a quality she had painstakingly fostered over years of spiritual seeking. It is apparent in her loyal answering of letters, however busy she was (I have two which are precious talismanic possessions).

Individuals felt it, as recollections by others testify. I did not meet her until after she had Alzheimer's and even that had not taken this quality away – I felt her full attention directed toward me, as if it was by then so ingrained a habit that illness had not stripped her of it. And John Bayley's account of her impact on audiences when she spoke also bears witness to the cultivation of total attention to the other, the stranger, the not-self:

> While never holding the floor she had the knack of taking seriously anything that was put forward by a questioner, and investigating its potential in a friendly and sympathetic way which was both flattering and rewarding for the audience. (Bayley, 147)

I think Iris Murdoch would laugh to hear herself described as good or saintly. She would ruefully remind me of her wry and ironic suggestion that 'be ye therefore perfect' was an unrealistic dominical demand, and that 'be ye therefore slightly improved' would have set a better goal (*EM*, 350). But I think she improved herself more than slightly through her efforts towards saintliness, even if perfection is beyond human grasp. Murdoch did much work on the spirit and offers her readers much work for the spirit. But she also knew the dark side of religious influence.

My slightly sinister ambiguous religious vein

This is a phrase from Iris Murdoch's journal, written on 15 June 1952 (*IMAL*, 451). It expresses the fascination that religion continued to have for her despite her intellectual rejection of doctrinal claims. Her distaste and mistrust will be made plain in her novels through the sometimes biting caricatures of clerical figures, and cameos of the damage which can be done to individuals by certain Christian perspectives and practices. But she will also create powerful pictures of people haunted by Christ and disquieted by God (as she herself continued to be). Religion, like sex, is one of the forms in which people assume power over others. It is in itself potentially sinister and ambiguous.

Certain of Iris Murdoch's novels explore the ill effects of religion: others the ill effects of the loss of religion. This is something that deeply concerned her:

> The general disappearance of religion from the background of the human mind is one of the most important things that have happened recently. [...] The disappearance of prayer from people's lives, the disappearance of any sort of practice of religion is [...] a sad phenomenon. (Dooley, 62)

Her novels depict our era as the time of the angels – spirit let loose in a world where God is dead – and suggest that this is an ambiguous and sinister time in which it is vital for the human race that we cling tenaciously, if grimly, to the concept of Good. This forms the nub of her philosophical programme, and it is to Iris Murdoch's philosophical journey that we now turn.

Chapter Four

The Mind: Philosopher, Teacher
and *Sartre, Romantic Rationalist*

She may break new ground.

John Wisdom[35]

There is savage irony in Alzheimer's being the disease that killed Iris Murdoch. Her brain was extraordinary and used to the full – which makes mockery of the notion that continuing to be mentally active will stave off Alzheimer's. This chapter focuses on Iris Murdoch's mind, on how she developed it during this period and on how impressive her original thinking was to the scholars who taught her and the students she taught. But first, we must again take a short retrospective of 'Previously in my life ...'

Iris Murdoch did well (though not brilliantly) in her Higher School Certificate (today's 'A' levels), passed the Oxford Entrance Examinations, and entered Somerville College in October 1938. She studied Classics (known as 'Greats') and gained a First Class degree in her Finals, taking papers on Logic, Morals and Politics, Plato and Aristotle, Ancient History, Greek History, Roman History, Prepared Translation, Unseens and Proses. When, years later, she applied for a job at St Anne's College, a shining report was given on her undergraduate prowess:

> As to <u>Miss Murdoch</u> there was no difficulty. The philosophers agreed that her logic paper (on which far the most weight is put) was first class. One philosopher thought all her work first class, the other thought there was first class quality visible in one other paper [...] she got her first without a viva and without any serious discussion. She was the only philosophy first to go straight in.[36]

The outbreak of war interrupted her formal intellectual progress, but it did not stop Iris Murdoch from reading and thinking. Meeting Sartre rekindled her latent desire to study philosophy and in April 1946, just six months after attending his lecture, she applied from her UNRRA camp to Newnham College, Cambridge for a Sarah Smithson Studentship. I spent a happy day in the Newnham College Archives, reading newly discovered letters they hold from and about Iris Murdoch. (One of the great joys of researching a biography is visiting archives and experiencing the visceral thrill of actually seeing and touching letters written by your subject – it gives an odd feeling of closeness to them across the years. Also the beautiful grounds of Newnham are lovely to picnic in when you take a break from transcribing.)[37]

When young she was already formidably learned.[38]

The document Iris Murdoch sent from Klagenfurt to Cambridge gives fascinating insight into how she was privately thinking and working whilst publicly performing her UNRRA duties.[39] She says 'I have of course read and thought a good deal, though not in a strictly disciplined manner, during the last four years', and defines her chief interest at Oxford as being 'theory of knowledge – particularly in what is broadly known as "Logical Positivism", in theories about language, (Vienna school of the Logical Positivists) and in the "analytical method" of dissolving problems, (Wittgenstein and Wisdom)'. But now her 'interest has shifted in the direction of ethics': she lacks sympathy with 'passionless formalistic theories' which fail to relate to 'the real moral problems' that distressed her and her contemporaries. Iris Murdoch describes these problems as 'all mixed up with emotion and psychology and religion and politics and all sorts of things that were not discussed': for the rest of her life she stuck with this mixed agenda and worked to get a multi-disciplinary approach to moral philosophy acceptable for discussion. The letter, written on the 9 April 1946, gives insight into her reading during this period. The work of Kierkegaard, Maritain and Buber convinced her that 'ethics could be seriously and profoundly treated from an academic point of view'. Buber and Dostoevsky are 'two striking landmarks'. She mentions the 'Existentialist' movement, Marcel and 'that strange genius Jean Paul Sartre' – she is reading *L'Etre et le Néant* at the time of writing. (She finished it 'with much admiration and some flutters of criticism' in July, and wrote to Queneau; 'it stops just where I want to begin; I suppose I shall now have to do some thinking for myself.')[40] In consequence of this formidable reading programme and the tough thinking she applied to all she read, at the age of twenty-six Iris Murdoch sets out her philosophical stall in an astonishingly assured tone:

> I feel the need to restate the problem [...] of human freedom and responsibility. What attracts me in the continental line of philosophers beginning with Kierkegaard and culminating in Sartre and Marcel is [...] their [...] attitude towards the existence of ethical questions, and their attempt to treat them, not insulated in an academic void, but from the point of view of the whole man.

Everything that is to come in her mature philosophy (and fiction) can be seen in embryo here.

However, Iris Murdoch's intellectual assurance was accompanied by personal uncertainty. She withdrew her application for the Sarah Smithson Studentship on being offered a Durant Drake Fellowship at Vassar College in New York State for which she simultaneously applied. But the USA would not permit her to study there because she admitted to having been a member of the Communist Party. (I cannot but wonder at this point at the part played by history and politics in the personal histories of individuals. Who would Iris Murdoch have become had she gone to America at this time? Speculation is fruitless but irresistible.) Emotionally deflated during the next impecunious year of lonely studying in her parents' house, Iris Murdoch lost the self-confidence she had felt in Austria. Re-applying to Newnham the following spring she wrote to Queneau:

> After much indecision about jobs, I've decided to apply for two next month – one a year-long studentship at Cambridge, and the other a lectureship in philosophy at Liverpool university, I don't know what my chances are for either. The Cambridge thing is to be applied for by June 1st [...] so that hanging on for that means letting go various jobs which I might chase after now. This thing is competitive however and I daresay I shan't get it. So – Liverpool, or else Bradford Technical Institute – or God knows what yet more frightful hack task in some redbrick town in some march in the midlands. (24 April 1947)

She need not have worried (*though she did not know this herself at the time* – the danger of the flash-forward in biography writing). Although they had already given the Studentship to another candidate, the College Council were so favourably impressed with Iris Murdoch's application that they offered a second one. She wrote of this self-deprecatingly as a 'piece of luck' (17 July 1947), rather than seeing it as her rightful due for not only having a brilliant mind but so energetically making use of it. Her differing self-perception is clear when she tells Queneau that she hopes for an academic job 'if it turns out that I can really think, which I am still in doubt about' (11 September 1946).

Iris Murdoch probably never saw the letters sent in support of her applications to Newnham. They would have buoyed her confidence: they also shed light on how she appeared to others at that period. Mildred Hartley, her tutor at Somerville College, wrote:

> I have had few pupils who got so much out of their University course as Miss Murdoch did, or made such good use of their opportunities. She had wide interests; she succeeded in subordinating the others to her work. She has immense energy & determination, great intellectual curiosity & staying power; she is critical, independent & fair-minded in discussion; she has personality & she has wisdom. She never shirked difficulties, & everything she wrote bore her individual stamp [...] since she went abroad in U.N.R.R.A. she has all the time pursued her intellectual interests, coming to concentrate more & more – & especially in the last two years – on philosophy [...] her work [...] & all my contact with her since she went down, leave me in no doubt that she is of first rate quality.[41]

The change in Iris Murdoch from the happy confident undergraduate is shockingly evident in the letter Donald MacKinnon, under whose supervision she was studying, sent on her behalf the following year:

> She seems to me quite peculiarly suited to study in Cambridge and [...] might produce work of real distinction. [...] I always thought her a student of real

promise, but she has recently matured considerably, and is now, I think, on the threshold of creative work of a high order. She has had a [...] rather bitter experience of life in the last few years, but has learnt from it a great deal that has made her disciplined and self critical.[42]

Her 'bitter experience' concerned men and rejection as well as war, grief and refugee camps. As Iris Murdoch insists, life is not compartmentalized: the emotional, physical, spiritual and intellectual are all interconnected. And all of this went with her to Cambridge in October 1947.

This university is so invigorating (intellectually speaking; the real climate is awful. Fogs & fens)[43]

So Iris Murdoch wrote to Queneau from her new home, 'The Pightle', a rather delightful postgraduate house she lived in during her year's studentship at Newnham. She shared the house with two 'students of botany from Auckland [....] Very nice girls, but talking to each other all the time about fungi' and a French lecturer Claude-Edmonde Magny who knew Queneau and of whom Iris Murdoch was in awe. She found it 'all very curious' both so like and so unlike her first year at Oxford (8 October 1947). Soon she confides that she feels 'most *depaysée*' in Cambridge and finds the philosophical atmosphere very unlike Oxford:

There is a scorn of any sort of scholarship in philosophy which I find very tiresome. For instance, hardly anyone bothers to read Kant or Hegel. The only subjects that are of real general interest are symbolic logic and the linguistic games [...] designed to remove 'worries' about problems which might seem metaphysical. No one is interested in ethics – except as a sort of butt for philosophical jokes! (14 October 1947)

This was a strange new environment for the serious and studious Iris Murdoch, to whom ethics was crucial. Dismissive Cambridge attitudes came as a shock to someone with such a passion for philosophy, whose enthusiasm bursts out in letter after letter to Queneau: 'just lately I have been having a great bout of Kant' (26 September 46); 'I must soon start trying to understand Hegel – that hiatus in my knowledge is proving intolerable' (11 September 1946), and 'I've been reading comrade Husserl (the "Ideen" in English) and find him very difficult and *très peu sympathetique* (sic) which probably just shows that I am *très peu philosophe* – I must try harder' (10 June 1947). On the eve of her entry into the dry world of Cambridge philosophy she told Queneau:

Sartre is exciting tho' – demonic. A sort of vertigo overcomes me, as if S. were repeating a spell: Be like me, be like me. I'm almost ready to say, yes, dammit, I am. But I'm not quite spellbound.

And, she admitted, 'Sometimes tho' I do see my philosophical pursuits as a process of intoxication. Some subtlety can be so voluptuous' (5 October 1947). Cambridge must have come like a cold shower.

I begin already to feel that I am a dreadful obscurantist [44]

Cambridge was a mixed blessing for Iris Murdoch. She wrote to Queneau, 'The landscape here is pretty barren, point of view people. Newnham is full of estimable and learned women with whom, so far as I can see, I shall be quite unable to communicate, except about the simplest banalities. [...] The need of someone with whom I can <u>communicate</u> is an anguish sometimes' (17 October 1947). She soon made new friends and had a rich social life. But intellectually she was isolated. Her ambivalence is plain when she tells Queneau: 'life is very pleasant and lively – but I still feel very lonely in what I'm trying to do, and not at all sure I'm capable of doing it' (29 October 1947). Lonely, uncertain and lacking in self-confidence – this is the Iris Murdoch of that era, the one I am trying to excavate from beneath the dazzling edifice of her successful double career.

Though painful, the intellectual challenge posed to Iris Murdoch was beneficial to her philosophical development. The rigorous demands made on her by the 'sportive logicians and mathematicians' (17 October 1947) of Cambridge and by her tutor John Wisdom, were a good corrective to the possible over-influence of Continental philosophy on her thinking at this stage. She liked John Wisdom who told her 'You don't learn philosophy as you learn chemistry – you learn it as you learn to play tennis'.[45] She took his point and moved surprisingly rapidly from telling Queneau that she doesn't care for symbolic logic, can't do it, and probably doesn't even know what it is (6 November 1947) to 'I feel a bit weary of existentialismus and even wish I could do some symbolic logic for a change' (6 November 1947).

Wittgenstein influenced Iris Murdoch strongly even though they passed one another like ships in the night as he left Cambridge (for Ireland) just weeks after her arrival there and she saw him only twice – she had already been reading his work for some years. That he caught her imagination is evident from his ghostly presence in her novels and from her philosophical wrestling match with his thought, concerning which she had a love-hate relationship. She worries away at him like a terrier with a rat. Ironically, when she returns to Oxford she is seen as a Wittgenstein expert – another of the jokes historical happenstance plays – and this impression remains in force today as Iris Murdoch is sometimes said to have studied under Wittgenstein.[46] Out of such errors, myths evolve.

Falling leaves and philosophical papers and broken hearts[47]

Iris Murdoch did not stay long in Cambridge even though she could have had a grant to do a Doctor of Philosophy thesis there had she wished. Feeling 'gloom and doubt' about her work she posed the central question to Queneau thus, 'can I really exploit the <u>advantages</u> (instead of as hitherto simply suffer from the disadvantages) of having a mind on the borders of philosophy, literature and politics' and told him, 'Every time I open a newspaper I wonder bitterly what on earth I'm up to' (17 October 1947). So she fled the fogs and fens and returned with relief to the 'rich honest slightly foggy arable countryside of Oxford' – philosophically as well as topographically.[48] Cambridge had not really suited her and she gladly took a teaching post at St Anne's College in October 1948. She had mentioned a 'very strong desire to teach philosophy' in her original letter from Klagenfurt, saying that 'teaching it would be learning it', worrying about the negative character of the teaching of philosophy at Oxford, and feeling it wrong 'to offer the young, who are ready for a rich diet of thought and emotion nothing but a cold technique of destructing'.[49] She was to get her chance to teach differently, and Oxford was delighted to have her back. Again, letters from the archives indicate the esteem in which she was held. John Wisdom expresses great confidence in Iris Murdoch's powers of mind and teaching potential:

She is an able woman with great subtlety and integrity of mind and her heart is in her work. She can use what others have done without losing her power to look at things for herself. All this makes me think that she will 'make a contribution to thought' in a way in which very few do. If she teaches she will put all of herself into it and those she teaches will like her I believe. They will have to face the good air of criticism but they will feel that it comes from someone with sympathy and understanding. I am confident that if she is appointed you will find the work you want done done well. (26 May 1948)[50]

While the Principal of her old college wrote to the Principal of St Anne's: 'Congratulations on Miss Murdoch, & many thanks for re-importing her into Oxford [...] a great acquisition & a most welcome one.'[51]

Teaching was demanding. In her first term Iris Murdoch wrote to Hal Lidderdale that she was 'quite overwhelmed with work. It's like being on a merry go round. Plato-Kant-Descartes-Moore-Plato-Kant-Berkeley-Sidgwick-Plato etc.' and she described her pupils as 'sweet [...] beautiful young women with new look skirts and red nails [...] not brilliant' (28 October 1948). She enjoyed teaching, liking both the subject and her pupils, but she found Oxford somewhat claustrophobic and often escaped to London – as she was to do for the rest of her life: 'The society gets me down in the long run tho! The donnishness of people, the cleverness – all the bleeding intellectuals. What a relief to board the London train and see those damn spires disappearing' (29 December 1948). She was resistant to becoming fully professionally socialized as an Oxford don, though John Bayley observes that 'like many philosophers in Oxford she had the habit of considering what was said in a silence that was judicious, almost sibylline' (Bayley, 21). Her passionate enthusiasm for philosophy had not abated; she exults to Queneau, 'Have got hold of *Sein und Zeit* at last & it lies in my room like an unexploded bomb' (18 March 1949). But she was struggling with it as she told him, 'I can't (at the moment) do philosophy [....] I find that I can't think. It's like turning a billiard ball in one's hands & trying to tear it open. I can't get started' (16 October 1949). In each case the image is as striking as the thought. Iris Murdoch brought her own original style to teaching philosophy. Her plan for an introductory lecture series includes, 'Ethical concepts: What does Wittgenstein mean in the *Tractatus* by saying that "ethics is transcendental"?' and 'Criticism of the existentialists' treatment of political and ethical concepts'.[52] Her tutorial teaching was not conventional. One of her pupils, Jennifer Dawson, remembers reading Political Theory with her, officially studying Hobbes, Rousseau and Aristotle's Politics. But Iris Murdoch was 'blithe and insouciante' about set texts and exams and 'roamed over philosophical ideas', being 'marvellously eclectic' and quoting 'from St Anselm and Engels in almost the same breath'. Dawson recalls that her eccentric tutor 'loved the earthy and concrete', had met Jean Paul Sartre, was mystical and influenced by existentialism and Simone Weil.[53]

Oxford was trying hard to ignore Existentialism. But the arrival of Iris Murdoch brought it firmly into the frame. She wrote tongue-in-cheek to Queneau: 'I'm just going back to Oxford, where I shall be lecturing on the existentialists, so the learned doctors in that city will be hearing the name of Sartre for the first time' (21 April 1953). She was only half-joking as Iris Murdoch wrote the first book about Sartre in English; she deserves credit for introducing Sartre and Existentialism to England. On 16 November 1953, John Bayley threw a party to celebrate the publication of Iris Murdoch's first book,

Sartre, Romantic Rationalist.[54] This monograph is a blend of literary criticism and moral philosophy, which mirrors the blurring of the boundaries between literature and philosophy characteristic of the writings of both Iris Murdoch and Sartre. Her feelings fluctuated. She jubilates to Hal Lidderdale, 'how <u>lovely</u> about existentialism-day! It has cheered me for weeks – and may be regarded as having been <u>celebrated</u>, in these regions at last!'[55] At other times she sounds weary of her subject: 'Must now return to the study of a bleak philosophy derived by a French atheist from a Danish mystic'.[56] Though Iris Murdoch's focus remained out of line with contemporaneous British philosophy, it also rapidly diverged from Continental philosophy as she gained her own original moral vision and her unique philosophical voice.

More lastingly significant than her book on Sartre, though, are the papers Iris Murdoch was producing at this time, and the discussions of which she became a part. As Justin Broackes remarks, she 'could hardly have been more enthusiastically received into the philosophical world' of Oxford.[57] Characteristically, Iris Murdoch *se lança même dans* (launched herself into) her new milieu, telling Queneau: 'Oxford is alright. The golden autumn suits it. I am trying to write three philosophical papers at once' (25 October 1950). And indeed, two reviews by her were published in the prestigious journal, *Mind*, in 1950. She attended the Joint Session of the Mind Association and the Aristotelian Society in July 1951 and made such an impression that she was (unusually) invited to give another talk in June 1952. She was keeping company with the leading philosophers of the time and holding her own. In 1956 – her *annus mirabilis* when she stayed in the decayed Anglo-Irish grandeur of Bowen's Court, published her second novel (proving that her first was not just a flash in the pan), married John Bayley and recorded in her journal the simplicity and joy of her new life – Iris Murdoch also published 'Vision and Choice in Morality', her 'first large-scale move into the field of moral philosophy'.[58] Her unremitting reading while working for UNRRA, her year of lonely private study in Chiswick and her exile to Cambridge had not been in vain. Chiefly by her own intellectual efforts, Iris Murdoch was becoming a philosophical force to be reckoned with. We must now backtrack, however, and return to where the thread is knotted, to see how Iris Murdoch's literary florescence ran in tandem (and in competition) with her philosophical development.

Chapter Five

The Heart: Novelist, Magician and *Under the Net*

The novel, that great sensitive mirror, or screen, or field of forces, is still one of the most articulate expressions of the dilemmas of its age.

Iris Murdoch[59]

If you ask the average person on the street who Iris Murdoch is, the answer would be 'a novelist'. In fact, I have distressingly discovered, the answer is, 'Who?' But the same is true if you enquire about Sartre or Dostoevsky (and certainly about Queneau or Weil). Literature and philosophy are minority pursuits. The masses who waited on the quays for Dickens's novels now mostly watch soap operas instead. But at the height of her popularity as a contemporary writer, the latest Iris Murdoch was eagerly awaited by at least the literati, and adverts featured people reading her novels. (Haydn and Donne both receded into obscurity before being resurrected by discerning musical and literary critics.) But if you follow Iris Murdoch on Twitter or Facebook you will find a lively conversation going on and undergraduates who specialize in her fiction today show the same passionate enthusiasm for her novels that I felt forty years ago. When the dust settles, literary history will record her as one of the greatest British novelists of the twentieth century.

I want one final time to repeat Iris Murdoch's remark to Queneau, quoted in chapters one and three, because it returns to her three deepest heart's desires:

> I think nothing is really worth anything except (a) being happily married, (b) being a saint, (c) writing a good novel. My chances of (a) diminish yearly, (b) is far too difficult – there remains (c) which still inspires hope. (16 March 1950)

She has (a). She is working hard and at least partially succeeding at (b). She was still inspired by hope for (c) – writing a good novel.

The only important thing

First, we must once more look briefly at 'Previously in my life ...'; to become a writer was Iris Murdoch's childhood ambition. But she served a long apprenticeship at her craft, just as Jane Austen and Virginia Woolf did. Art and ethics always went hand in hand for Iris Murdoch. Her application to Cambridge from the

UNRRA camp states, 'I have written a good deal during the last four years – never anything which could be called a philosophical treatise, but novels rather and dialogues, dealing [...] with definite moral problems' (9 April 1946). She was always trying to write a novel alongside her work on philosophy and, paradoxically, she both lacked confidence in her talent and firmly believed that she would succeed. The note of uncertainty is strong in letters to her literary mentor Queneau: 'I must try another novel soon. Anything I shall ever write will owe so much, so much to you. I wish I knew if I could write – shall find out by trying no doubt' (15 February 1947). She wrote four or five novels which she never published – and subsequently destroyed – and she gives tantalizing glimpses of these still-born works:

I have started writing the novel about the Bogus Scholar and the Archaic Goddess which has been in my head so long, but doubt if I'll finish it before the autumn. I'll show it you, if it ever gets done. In idea at least, it's a bit Queneau-esque. In execution – I don't know. (17 July 1947)

She went on trying out new ideas for fiction during her year in Cambridge:

I've asked a bookseller to send you Carrington's 'Telepathy' which may amuse you. His theory, though wrong I've no doubt, is interesting. (The

novel I am writing – or 'writing' – now is based on an
idea cribbed from Carrington!) (25 November 1947.)

Lecturing and teaching philosophy at Oxford frustratingly
stole time from her fictional efforts, 'My current novel
has been abandoned a long time now' (17 February
1952). But she always had one on the go, and that it
never ceased to be a matter of primary importance for
her is clear from this despairing cry to Queneau, 'When
I shall write a novel again I don't know & this after all is
the only important thing' (13 March 1951).

This short biography focuses on the period in her life
when, despite her self-doubts and crises of confidence, Iris
Murdoch achieved her dream and succeeded in becoming
a novelist. Returning literature to the centre of her
endeavours, after deviating down the path of philosophy,
was in fact returning to where Iris Murdoch began. Her
place at Somerville College was originally awarded to
read English Literature – she changed to Greats in her
first term. Again, historical accident plays a part. Had
she found Mary Lascelles, the Jane Austen scholar who
was the formidable English tutor at Somerville at that
time, more *sympatique*, Iris Murdoch might have stuck
with her first choice of discipline and we would not have
the innovative challenging philosophical texts as well as
the novels. Though it is hard to imagine one without the
other, so closely do literature and philosophy intertwine
in her *oeuvre*. During these years, her interest in literature
played second fiddle, because she was employed to teach
philosophy, but, though she distinguishes clearly between
the two discourses, Iris Murdoch always held firmly to

her sense of the importance of literature to philosophical thinking. Her plan for an introductory series of lectures included 'What is a great novelist doing, and what new experience does he give us?'[60]

During these years Iris Murdoch is torn between her passion for literature and her passion for philosophy; they vie for her time and attention. Uncertainty and guilt combine in her letters to Queneau:

> For some time now I have been writing a novel, a continuation of one I started two years ago. If it turns out to be any use (about this I still don't know) I shall dedicate it to you. But I daresay it won't ever see the light. And for this I have stopped reading Hegel's Logic. (4 August 1952).

She delves into literary theory at the expense of reading philosophical texts: 'I am running around with literary criticism at present – Richards and Leavis etc – principles of. Pure being & the synthetic a *priori* are getting on without me' (31 May 1950). She reads voraciously in English and European literature, delighting in fresh discoveries, 'I've just finished reading *Tom Jones* which I'd never read before. What a delicious book – and how good to read an author who writes so well with such relish. I feel more robust already' (14 September 1952). She yearns wistfully after a career in literature, telling Queneau: 'If I could see a means of doing it I'd slip over from philosophy into English Literature – but this is difficult, probably impossible' (13 March 1951). She tells Queneau that she has contracted to write a short book on 'Sartre, Camus & de Beauvoir as <u>novelists</u>' (31 May 1950) – her emphasis, and her first published work, *Sartre, Romantic Rationalist* is as much a work of literary criticism as of philosophy.

Iris Murdoch developed the view that 'A good critic is a relaxed polymath' (*EM*, 24), and she married such a man: John Bayley, who was – in his own words – in the 'Eng. Lit. Business' (Bayley, 52) and who was to become the Warton Professor of English and write fine scholarly essays and monographs. (Significantly, the first thing Iris Murdoch confided to him when they became acquainted was that she had written a novel.) They were reading companions who shared each other's worlds and could discuss authors and debate ideas together. John Bayley's memoirs of Iris Murdoch contain, slipped lightly and unobtrusively between pages of anecdote and reflection, incisive critical commentary on his wife's novels which illuminate her mysterious imagination and fecundity. But at this point in her life, she did not even know if she would ever get a novel published.

Exercises in disappointment

Iris Murdoch uses this phrase in a letter to Queneau (perhaps echoing his title *Exercises in Style*) but she goes on to say stoically, 'Anyway, how adaptable one is! (I find), like those newt embryos that biologists like to torment' (15 February 1947). Life seemed to be tormenting her at this point. Iris Murdoch had known rejection of her work from publishers, as well as of herself from men.

It is small wonder that her self-confidence was at a low ebb; more remarkable really is her dogged perseverance. After each failed attempt, with novels as with lovers, she picked herself up, dusted herself off, and started all over again. In November 1944 the second novel Iris Murdoch had written was rejected by no less than T.S. Eliot at Faber & Faber; in November 1946 John Lehmann rejected her labour of love, the translation of Queneau's *Pierrot mon ami*, which, as we saw in chapter one, was a deep disappointment to her. It was some time before she regained the confidence to risk further rebuff and she was sternly self-critical. In October 1949 Iris Murdoch abandoned another novel, about a spiritual seeker in Tibet called *Our Lady of the Bosky Gates*, and began to work on *Under the Net* – which as yet had no title. Shortly afterwards she contracted with Bowes & Bowes to write her book on the French Existentialist novelists (which was never accomplished though her work on it fed into *Sartre, Romantic Rationalist*) and she gave two radio talks on the Third Programme which were subsequently published in *The Listener*, 'The Novelist as Metaphysician' and 'The Existentialist Hero'. She was refining what was important to her by analysing the work of other novelists. The first draft of what was to become *Under the Net* was finished in March 1953 and she immediately started to contemplate another novel which was brewing in her imagination and would become the second published, *The Flight from the Enchanter*. (This title likewise was not chosen until later, a new draft written the following July is called *The Education of Annette*.) Throughout her life, Iris Murdoch would work in parallel on different novels, ideas for the next blossoming in her mind before the previous one was published. There is thus a leap-frog dynamic to her creative writing rhythm.

Starting a novel is opening a door on a misty landscape; you can still see very little but you can smell the earth and feel the wind blowing. I could feel the wind blowing from the first pages [...] and it blew strongly and tasted fresh [61]

Whatever emotional harm he may have done her, Canetti played a vital role in Iris Murdoch's literary fortunes as it was he who sent the manuscript of her first novel to Viking, who in August 1953 sent it to Chatto & Windus who were to publish all her novels. Meanwhile Iris Murdoch, unable to foretell her own future, continued writing *The Flight from the Enchanter* without knowing what the fate of her first novel was to be. On 3 October 1953 she learned the outcome, and – a rare occurrence – noted the outset of her literary career in her journal. Both Chatto & Windus and Viking had accepted *Under the Net* for publication. The years of waiting were over and her persistence was rewarded. In the interim before *Under the Net* was published on 20 May 1954, Iris Murdoch wrote her only short story, *Something Special*, inspired by a brief visit to Ireland that Easter. As she had always promised, she dedicated her first published novel to Raymond Queneau who had been her inspiration for so long and whose letters had encouraged her not to give up trying. 'I wish I could put my learning into novels, as you do. Sea-changed of course into the rich and strange' (5 October 1947), she had written to him so many years before and now she too was doing just this. Queneau's opinion still mattered hugely to Iris Murdoch. She was hurt at the lack of excitement he showed at her dedicating her first novel to him, and there is still an undercurrent of lack of self-confidence in her reply to his letter of praise: 'Thank you for your very nice letter about Under the Net. The thing has had pretty good criticism here, & one or two attacks from people who couldn't stand it at any price', she says and then, scribbled diagonally across the fourth page after her signature, she adds, 'It pleases me very much that you like Under the Net. I hope you really do. I should be very sad if you didn't' (26 June 1954).

The literary forbears of *Under the Net* are Queneau's *Pierrot mon ami* and Samuel Beckett's *Murphy* (which Iris Murdoch read as an undergraduate – she wrote Beckett a fan letter in 1939), to both of which she freely acknowledged her debt. Also Sartre's *La Nausée*, about which she was more reserved, anxious not to be thought a philosophical novelist like him and de Beauvoir. Iris Murdoch's début novel does not fit tidily into one genre: it has elements of the picaresque and the *bildungsroman*, it has been described as a self-begetting novel by Steven Kellman and scholars are still contending, despite Iris Murdoch's prohibitions, that it is, in some form or another, a philosophical novel. Wittgenstein's spirit is certainly present. But it is not a heavy novel, it has the deceptive lightness of a *jeu d'esprit*, the pace is fast, the tone witty. It is extremely funny. And although its setting in post-war London has passed into history (new buildings raised on the bombed-out wastelands, a new Millennium Bridge at the point where the narrator Jake enters the Thames for a midnight swim) *Under the Net* has not dated. It reads as freshly today as it did sixty years ago.

Trial and error had convinced Iris Murdoch that her most successful narrative mode was male first-person. There is no critical consensus on which is the 'best' of her novels (each reader has personal favourites) but three of the six novels she wrote from this perspective are among the most highly acclaimed, *The Black Prince* and *The Sea, The Sea* – which won her the Booker Prize in 1978 – as well as the first, *Under the Net*; (the other three are *A Severed Head*, *The Italian Girl* and *A Word Child* which is one of my own personal favourites). Jake Donaghue is something of a Sartrean anti-hero and it was this – along with the novel's comedy – which caused contemporary reviewers to class Iris Murdoch with John Brain, Kingsley Amis, John Osborne *et al* as one of the 'Angry Young Men', an assessment which retrospectively is clearly nonsensical. But she did attain the same overnight success of her contemporary male writers. *Under the Net* was well received and quickly became popular. It was selected as 'Book of the Month' in the *Newcastle Journal* which rarely chose a first novel. It was the runner-up at the Cheltenham Literature Festival in October that year – beaten only by Brigid Brophy's début novel, *Hackenfeller's Ape*, and the judges were so impressed by *Under the Net* that they specially created a second prize to acknowledge its merit. (Another point in Iris Murdoch's life where happenstance has repercussions: it was at this event that she met Brigid Brophy who features in her complicated personal life discussed in chapter two. Literary work and sex do not inhabit sealed compartments in life.)

By February 1955 the second draft of *The Flight from the Enchanter* was completed and in August-September that year Iris Murdoch wrote the first draft of her third novel which was to be called *The Sandcastle*. In between, in March 1955, John Bayley published *his* first novel, *In Another Country*, and gave Iris Murdoch a copy with the inscription 'Horror-Comic for IM from JB'. Marrying her was to inhibit his creative writing, however, and he wrote no further novels until she herself had ceased to write because of the effects of Alzheimer's. Then he felt that she had handed the baton on to him and in the 1990s he rapidly wrote four more, as if his imagination had just been waiting for release; a trilogy, *Alice*, *The Queer Captain* and *George's Lair*, and finally, *The Red Hat*. In January 1956 Iris Murdoch finished the second draft of *The Sandcastle*, which had taken her only four months to write, and on 23 March *The Flight from the Enchanter* was published, dedicated to the Arch-Enchanter figure in her own life, Elias Canetti. Iris Murdoch married John Bayley that August, as we have seen, and *The Sandcastle*, dedicated to her new husband, was published on 7 May 1957.

At last, after a faltering start, Iris Murdoch had succeeded in becoming a novelist. Exploding onto the literary scene with *Under the Net*, then following that up with, in such rapid succession, *The Flight from the Enchanter* and *The Sandcastle*, she was off like a race horse, a ship in full sail, a mountain skier, and she didn't stop writing for another forty years until Alzheimer's took her mind away from her. Conradi astutely describes Murdoch's first novels as 'five different débuts'.[62] In 1958 *The Bell* surprised reviewers with its treatment of religion and homosexuality and it remains one of her best loved works, made into a film by the BBC in 1981.[63] *A Severed Head* surprised not only readers of the novel but also audiences of the play into which Iris Murdoch and J.B. Priestley adapted it in 1963, by its 'sexual square dance' which includes incest. (Iris Murdoch was disappointed when an attempt by a film company to make a film of *Under the Net* came to nought.)

This short biography is purposefully restricted to that decade of Iris Murdoch's life when she was a work in progress, busy becoming herself – as a wife, a seeker after Good, a philosopher, and above all as a novelist – so I am not going to follow her career any further, but leave her here as a fully established and acclaimed author. Readers who want to know more about her novels can find the full list in the appendix. The main questions I want to ask now concern: 1) What kind of fiction did Iris Murdoch write? 2) How did becoming a novelist affect her? 3) Why is the novel in the end her chosen form? This was the genre to which she devoted the bulk of her time and energy for the rest of her life, at the expense of the philosophy which she also continued to love and write about.

Iris has always had – must have had – so vast and rich and complex an inner world [64]

There is no single or simple answer to the first of

these questions. The literary world divides into those who think her fiction is frankly Bad and will vanish into deserved oblivion, and those who think it is exceptionally Good and will pass into the Canon (if such a concept continues to be meaningful in the twenty-first century). The second group sub-divides almost indefinitely with heterogeneous views expressed in books, essays, conference papers and conversations about *what* is good about Iris Murdoch's fiction and *why* it is good. To give a flavour of it I choose John Bayley – rather than any of the renowned Iris Murdoch scholars to whom this book is too short to do justice – as spokesman for the defence. He lived alongside her as she wrote and is one of the most widely read and perceptive literary critics of the twentieth century. John Bayley's key word is the 'world' of Iris Murdoch. He knows that:

> She wanted, in her novels, to reach all possible readers, in different ways and by different means: by the excitement of her story, its pace and its comedy, through its ideas and its philosophical implications, through the numinous atmosphere of her own original and created world. (25-6)

He sees this as 'the world she must have glimpsed as she considered and planned her first steps in the art of fiction' (26). This is what she was working to create, to explore in her head and express in words, during those eleven years of her life to which this biography is dedicated. In his commentary on 'her own marvellous world of creation and intellectual drama, penetrating reflection, sheer literary excitement' (37), John Bayley thinks that Iris Murdoch's 'free world in her novels [...] carries total conviction because it is like no other, and like no one else's' and that this 'is why this world has such mesmeric appeal for all sorts of different people' (160). His summation of the value of his wife's fiction relates it to her personality – or rather, to its absence in her novels:

> Iris's works, at least to me, are genuinely mysterious, like Shakespeare's. About her greatness as a novelist I have no doubts at all, although she has never needed, possessed or tried to cultivate the charisma which is the most vital element in the success of a sage or mage. Her books create a new world, which is also in an inspired sense an ordinary one. They have no axe to grind; they are devoid of intellectual pretension, or the need to be different. They are not part of a personality which fascinates and mesmerises its admirers. Although any of her readers might say or feel that a person or an event in her fiction could only occur in a Murdoch novel, and nowhere else, this does not mean that the personality of the writer herself is in any obvious sense remarkable. (120)

The issue of the author's personality in – or absence of it from – her work relates to the imperative for unselfing discussed in the context of religion in chapter three. Just as the good person becomes, in Iris Murdoch's view, less and less visible, so the good writer does not obtrude into her work.

Becoming a novelist encouraged, intensified and

validated Iris Murdoch's tendency (shared perhaps by all novelists) to live in an imaginary world of her own making. I think that the chief effect that her success had on her was to allow her to withdraw into that world. John Bayley suggests this when he says that 'her novels, and her ceaseless invention, from day to day and month to month, were where she lived' (131) and wonders whether her 'stream of consciousness' – something he is very aware of in his own case but which Iris Murdoch denied having – all went 'into the world of creation, which lived inside her' (172). I think writing novels also made Iris Murdoch very happy – though John Bayley mentions that she was always 'gloomy [...] about any novel she had done with' (151), for she felt that each novel was the wreck of a perfect idea. She could never quite capture the vision she wanted to encapsulate and she could never measure up to the nineteenth-century realist novelists she revered.

It was those works, which make space for 'free characters', which gave Iris Murdoch such a high doctrine of the novel and made it for her a moral as well as aesthetic concern. She believes that 'a great novelist [...] displays a real apprehension of persons other than the author as having a right to exist and to have a separate mode of being which is important and interesting to themselves', and that *love* is the best name 'for this capacity at its highest' (*EM*, 271, 283). (Close parallels between her statements of this nature and John Bayley's study *The Characters of Love* indicate their mutual influence on each other's thinking.)[65] *Metaphysics as a Guide to Morals*, her last long philosophical work, contains the assertion: 'Good novels concern the fight between good and evil and the pilgrimage from appearance to reality. They expose vanity and inculcate humility. They are amazingly moral' (*MGM*, 97). She further believes that 'experience of the art of the novel is spiritual experience' (*EM*, 282). Becoming a novelist and spending her life writing fiction certainly proved a spiritual experience for Iris Murdoch, and many will testify that reading her novels can be exactly that too.

Art is very much to do with accident, with contingency, with detail, with self-expression, with trickery of all kinds, with magic [66]

But reading her novels is also a magical experience. Iris Murdoch sees and fears the potential for magic in metaphysics and religion: she accepts its presence as an integral element in art. By contrast with philosophy, she says literature is 'for fun' and 'is full of tricks and magic and deliberate mystification' *(EM*, 4). Magician characters feature in her fiction and she knows the novelist herself is a magician, a Prospero figure. This is an ambivalent role for her to play. Having escaped from enchantment herself, Iris Murdoch was wary about being an enchantress to others, even to readers. She both delights in and mistrusts the magical power of her fiction.

Conclusion

The Flight from Becoming the Enchantress

It is not what one has experienced but what one does with what one has experienced that matters.[67]

Apologia Pro Biographia Sua

Writing a biography, I discover, feels very presumptuous. What gives me the right to comment on someone else's life? And why do I want to tell her story? These questions return to the motivation of biographers which this book began by considering. Biography might be written to celebrate a life, to set the record straight or to put on record facts previously unknown. Alternatively, biography might be written to hand on to others the passion one feels for one's subject and her achievements – I think that is as close as I can come. But how can I know that what I say is true? I think that is why I have wanted to let so much of the story be told by Iris Murdoch and John Bayley in their own words. But how do I know *those* words are true, either? Just as I feel I may have made Iris Murdoch up I fear that she might have made her story up too. That is why there is such a sense of beatitude in finding *her* account of where and when and how they met so perfectly corroborated by Queneau's *Journaux*: it forms a kind of cross-reference that plots the event securely on the historical map. As also do the letters and reports on Iris Murdoch's career found in archives in Cambridge and Oxford.

Biographers, I find, have to factor in doubt. John Bayley admits the pitfalls of the task of recollection to which he felt compelled, pitfalls which apply to this work of my own as to all biographical writing:

> No description of anybody, however loving, can seem to do anything but veer away from the person concerned, not because it distorts their 'reality', whatever that may be, but because the describer himself begins to lose all confidence in the picture of the person he is creating. The Iris of my words cannot, I know, be any Iris who existed. (Bayley, 104)

Henry James, whose work both Iris Murdoch and John Bayley loved, exclaims, 'The art of the biographer – devilish art! – is somehow practically *thinning*. It simplifies even while seeking to enrich'.[68] This is a sad truth in each individual case, but the built up layers of each biographical foray ('a wholly new start and a different kind of failure')[69] may also hopefully create a *thickening* palimpsest of interpretation.

Even if one uses original source material, it is still tampered with by the time it reaches the page. I have selected which letters, which *phrases* from those letters, removed them from context, rearranged them in patterns that fit my own agenda for what I want to say about Iris Murdoch. She herself casts doubt on the trustworthiness of letters. She tells Lidderdale, 'This bad letter, which doesn't really seem to speak with my voice, is just to reach out to you' (29 June 1951), and writes to Queneau, 'This letter feels a bit off the mark. Not quite what I want to say. There are better things, honester, deeper maybe, that don't get said' (6 November 1947). Further, she admits to him that she has 'imagined various replies (insouciant, désespéré, etc' (17 February 1952). Selection of the facts thus begins even before the primary sources are created. Iris Murdoch's secretiveness makes me wonder yet more at the possibility of veracity. She confesses to Lidderdale concerning her relationship with Hicks, 'You will ask why the hell I never told you about this – a grave *suppressio veri*' (28 February 1946). John Bayley was none too sure of her opacity either:

> In her first published novel, *Under the Net*, it is remarked of the leading female character that she never lets on to any one of her friends just how closely bound she is to all the rest of them [...] That was true of Iris. (Bayley, 15)

Perhaps all a biographer can do is be open about the gaps in her knowledge and as honest as possible (there are levels of self-deception of which one is not even aware) about the slant she is putting on her personal account of her subject – as I declared at the start, this is *my* Iris Murdoch I have been telling you about.

I have called this book *Becoming Iris Murdoch* as it focuses on the formative period of her life when she was becoming the great writer whom we know. It ends with all the elements of her future – marriage, teaching and writing – in place. But later in her life the process was perhaps strangely reversed, for as she practised the unselfing that her philosophy advocates she started what one might call 'un-becoming'. Maybe that has to be another book – about the end of her life. For now I want to review the impression made by these early years.

I wish I had a spare lifetime to spend in Paris[70]

The most dominant thing which strikes me as I explore every aspect of Iris Murdoch's existence is her sheer vitality. Her novels bubble and fizz with joyous energy and so did she – one of the characteristics that made (and still makes) her so seductively attractive. A bias I am aware this account is guilty of, is an over-emphasis on the negative, caused by wanting to explore how it felt to her before she attained her goals and when *she did not know that she was going to succeed*. My picture of Iris Murdoch may be unbalanced by this. At the same time as being uncertain and lonely, she was also full of youthful high spirits, *delighting* in her travels and adventures, affairs and liaisons, and *relishing* her reading and thinking, writing and arguing. She loved life, and it is a flaw in my approach if that exuberance has been disregarded. The sheer energy with which Iris Murdoch *se lança même dans* (how absolutely that French phrase encapsulates her approach) everything that life could offer is breathtaking. I am struck by how *busy* she is all the time. To Lidderdale she writes with unconscious irony, that there is 'little news of me' before going on to tell him: 'I am at Chiswick, trying to finish a trivial thing on Sartre. Next week I go to Edinburgh to read a paper to an Aristotelian Society gathering. [...] Lectures for next term, the horrid Sartre thing, perhaps a novel I abandoned 18 months ago' (29 June 1951). Little news indeed! She has so many projects on the go at once, telling Queneau: 'I am feverishly completing the book on Sartre & de Beauvoir <u>romanciers</u> [...] Then I must write this Aristotelian society paper on Thinking and Language' (22 December 1951). And all this against a background of teaching and lecturing, never mind running a cat's cradle of friendships and love affairs. Yet she isn't satisfied with what can be accomplished in a single lifetime, full though she packs it. She longs for another life to live in France, cries out to Queneau, 'isn't time <u>terrible</u>, isn't it an absolute torment' (10 August 1952), and 'What a pity one can't really read dozens of books at once' (15 November 1947).

The evil that men do lives after them, the good is often interred with their bones[71]

Notwithstanding her own chagrin, Iris Murdoch achieved a quite phenomenal amount. She lived every aspect of her life to the full, exploring her own promiscuity and sado-masochism, her yearning for the holy and transcendent, her passion for philosophy and ethics, and – above all – her burning drive to write novels, to create art. This biography ends as she was really just beginning. She went on to write a further twenty-one novels and to make a weighty contribution to moral philosophy, which is only now in the twenty-first century beginning to be properly valued. She is now becoming established as an important writer in a changed philosophical climate – but her work helped inaugurate that change. Iris Murdoch left her brain to science for research into Alzheimer's. But she bequeathed her mind to her readers – in her novels, and also in the pages of *Existentialists and Mystics* and *Metaphysics as a Guide to Morals*. Here it is as if her thoughts are extracted like Dumbledore's 'pensieve' in *Harry Potter*. These are uneven but richly rewarding volumes: the distillation of a lifetime of reading, brooding, musing, meditating, contemplating, thinking and feeling.

Iris Murdoch's career as both novelist and moral philosopher enacts a duality embodied within her. I think it was when she herself became uncomfortably aware of this internal divison that she both started to work at becoming good through unselfing, and was also liberated to write fiction. Her art deals with morals – just as the rather prim-sounding young woman declares in her application letter to Newnham ('I have written [...] novels [...] dealing [...] with definite moral problems') – but moral problems made so human and so humorous that there is nothing prim or heavy about her fiction, which laughs its way to the truth. As she says in that self-revelatory letter, her subject is not abstract idealised man, but:

> man with blood in his veins, and a complicated psychology (and partly conscious of it) and with definite social and emotional problems to face – the man who goes to the cinema, makes love, and fights for or against Hitler. (9 April 1946)

It is such men (and women) who people her novels. And it is (sometimes bitter and remorseful) self-knowledge which enabled her to create them in full humanity, with badness and goodness intermingled.

For Iris Murdoch's amoral behaviour at times is in sharp contrast with her acute moral awareness: this forms a split in her identity which she exploits to the full. As a philosopher and as a moral person she wants to be good: as a novelist she wants to know and experience all. Furthermore, as a philosopher, Iris Murdoch is demandingly absolute; morality and personal responsibility have no stopping place. As an artist she is both wryly realistic about human moral capacities and optimistic concerning the perpetual resurgence of moral sensibility in human life. She sets the concepts of freedom and determinism against one another in individual cases which her novels vividly dramatize. So while her philosophy robustly confronts and challenges us, her fiction more gently explains and enlightens us.

Iris Murdoch made her own life the crucible of experience for her fiction. When Franz died she wrote in genuine agony to Queneau, 'Days pass full of devices for avoiding being in pain' (13 December 1952). She uses the knowledge of grief which she thus painfully gained to great effect in her novels which offer case studies of bereavement and remorse. She likewise uses her knowledge of sexual domination and submission to paint terrible and hilarious pictures of human relationships in all their cruelty, tenderness and bizarre particularity. 'Art,' she knew well, 'is to do with sex and with the unconscious mind' (*EM*, 247).

Fertile confusions are developing[72]

It is impossible to pigeon-hole Iris Murdoch's fiction, labelling (as some still persist in trying to do) individual novels as 'philosophical-novels', or as novels about sex or about religion. They are *all* about all of these things and a good deal more besides – the whole range and richness of human experience – creatively integrated in 'fertile confusion'. She told Queneau:

> I started life as a political animal thinking my soul didn't matter – now I am almost a religious animal, thinking it matters vitally. In the swing between those two attitudes lie all the philosophical problems that interest me. (26 September 1946)

Sex too, in Iris Murdoch's thinking, is mixed in with everything else, because what she terms Eros, 'pictures probably a greater part of what we think of as "the moral life"; that is, most of our moral problems involve an orientation of our energy and our appetites' (*MGM*, 497). At the same time, she says, 'Everything I have ever written is concerned with holiness',[73] and her chosen stopping place for *Metaphysics as a Guide to Morals* is Psalm 139. 'Whither shall I go from thy spirit, whither shall I flee from thy presence [...] even there shall thy hand lead me, and thy right hand shall hold thee' (512).

John Bayley tells us that the question of identity puzzled Iris Murdoch. By the time they discussed it, the unselfing or 'un-becoming' process may have made this true. But it would have been disingenuous of Iris Murdoch during the portion of her life which this book chiefly covers to have made any such claims. A person without a sense of identity does not write such letters (with separately constructed personae for different correspondents – the Proteus-effect). Nor does she keep journals. On the contrary, the young Iris Murdoch had a very strong sense of identity, or rather of identities; sexual, spiritual, intellectual and creative. It took her until marriage and maturity to begin to fuse these identities and subsume them into her fiction. After marriage (which she so longed for) she had the space to write, and in writing she maybe lost or forgot her younger sense of identity. Emotionally stable and domestically comfortable at last with John Bayley, she could vanish into the imaginative world inside of her head – the world of her novels.

Without John Bayley Iris Murdoch would not have become who she was. Parallels between their marriage and the fruitful happy literary partnership of the Woolfs are drawn in Olivia Laing's charmingly whimsical book, *To the River: A Journey Beneath the Surface*:

> This marriage, in which a clever and kindly man takes care of his more brilliant wife, bears a distinct resemblance to that of Leonard & Virginia Woolf, who also lived rather sluttily [....] Grubbiness aside [...] it's something about the mechanics of the two relationships, for they each resemble delicate instruments that rely on careful weighting and a judicious use of space. Both women were pulled in two opposing directions throughout their lives: inward, towards the intense, almost febrile life of the mind; and outward, towards a mélange of external love affairs and passions. Despite this both felt their husbands to be the steady centre of their lives [....] The two couples nurtured a kind of fertile separateness, a *solitude à deux*.[74]

A further parallel is suggested by Harris's statement that although 'there is much that is controversial' about Virginia Woolf 'she makes one want to live more consciously and fully.' (Harris, 9) I echo that with regard to Iris Murdoch. A.S. Byatt has said that since knowing Iris Murdoch she has been unable to tell a lie. As a young woman Iris Murdoch meant to make her mark: she has certainly left her mark on A.S. Byatt, myself and countless others.

How Iris Murdoch Can Change Your Life
(with apologies to Alain de Botton)

John Bayley recalls a newspaper interviewer telling Iris Murdoch that 'she had found out all about herself, while she had found out nothing about Iris' (126). I find out much about myself through reading Iris Murdoch's work and have done so again in the process of writing this book. How much I have found out about Iris Murdoch, beyond certain historical facts, is a moot point. I have given a portrait of her in these pages, as she seems to me, but I don't know how much resemblance it bears. John Bayley writes of different Irises:

> The Iris with whom I talked nonsense and gambolled about, the woman who entered with such joy into those frolics [...] was not the same woman I had first seen and marked out: nor was she the 'real' Iris Murdoch, the serious hard-working responsible being observed and admired by other people. (Bayley, 40)

Conradi observes that Iris Murdoch 'repeatedly asked herself "What is it like?" of many disparate phenomena' [75] and I suppose that I, like John Bayley, am trying to answer the question: what is Iris Murdoch like? But can one ever answer that about another person (even about oneself)? Her philosophy and fiction both stress that the individual is unutterably particular and demand 'moral attitudes which emphasize [...] the importance of not

117

assuming that one has got individuals and situations "taped"' (*EM*, 87). So perhaps all I dare say is; Iris Murdoch loved wine and art, London and Dorset, dogs and spiders, Shakespeare and Tolstoy, Paris and Provence, her husband and friends, Titian and Tintin, stones and trees. Like all great artists, she knew remorse. She brings the world to life in her pages. She makes you *see*. She makes you *think*.

Readers enter books only to be entered by them[76]

I feel about Iris Murdoch as she felt about Raymond Queneau, 'Your mind is a country which I find very agreeable'. I met Iris Murdoch the novelist when my dad gave me *The Unicorn* to read as a teenager. Intoxicated by the golden whiskey haze and the heady mix of eroticism and spirituality, I had a sense of something there to get my teeth into as well as finding it compellingly readable. I went on to *The Flight from the Enchanter* and was hooked. Forty years later, I still am. Something Iris Murdoch says about Proust can equally be applied to her own work, 'In writing the book Proust has of course revealed himself [...] as every great novelist does, as a great moralist as well as a great artist' (*MGM*, 263). Like Proust, Iris Murdoch is both. Edward Baltram in *The Good Apprentice* reads *À la recherche du temps perdu*:

What a lot of pain there was in those first pages. What a lot of pain there was all the way through it. So how was it that the whole thing could vibrate with

such pure joy? This was something which Edward
was determined to find out. (*GA*, 560)

It is something which I constantly try to find out with
regard to Iris Murdoch's novels too.

Light is cast for me on why I find her work so powerful
by a Turkish novelist, Orhan Pamuk, (whose work I read
when going to Istanbul to lecture on Iris Murdoch – there
are surprising parallels). Pamuk astutely remarks that
'All great novels open your eyes to things you already
knew but could not accept, simply because no great novel
had yet opened your eyes to them'[77]. And, further:

A wondrous novel becomes an integral part of our
lives and the world around us, bringing us closer
to the meaning of life; it comes in place of that
happiness we may never find in living to offer us a
joy that derives from its meaning. (Pamuk, 115-6)

Iris Murdoch's wondrous novels are such an integral part
of my life.

I had thought to end this book – another difficulty of
biography writing which I have discovered through this
experimental attempt is how do you conclude, especially
when you leave your subject mid-life and flourishing – by
keeping my promise to recount my one meeting with Iris
Murdoch, the only unknown fact I have to contribute
to the picture of her life. It is a very short tale. When I
read *Jackson's Dilemma*, hot off the press, I was troubled
as so many readers were. Something was not right. Then
John Bayley released the news that she had Alzheimer's.

Saddened by realizing that I would never now have that imagined conversation with her about her novels, I wanted to make a futile gesture of love, so – rather cornily – I bought an armful of irises at the Covered Market in Oxford and went to her house. I expected to leave them with John Bayley with a mumbled message of appreciation, but Iris Murdoch herself opened the door. She received the flowers graciously and while I stammered some inadequate words, she took my hand in hers – it was warm – and she smiled directly into my eyes. I know that she probably dropped the irises in the dust behind the front door and forgot my visit before I had even reached the gate but it was indeed like being in the angelic presence of goodness.

But that ends the book with the biographer's tale, and I want to give the biographee the last word. Which of the millions she wrote over her lifetime should it be? She is so quotable. I walk in and out of her novels as if they were rooms in my head and I have so many favourite passages and incidents – the joy of meeting other Iris Murdoch readers is that they know who you are talking about immediately. Her central credo has always seemed to me to be summed up in this short pithy fragment:

Art and morals are, with certain provisos [...] one. Their essence is the same. The essence of both of them is love. Love is the perception of individuals. Love is the extremely difficult realisation that something other than oneself is real. Love, and so art and morals, is the discovery of reality. (*EM*, 215)

But I think I should leave you with Iris Murdoch's hymn in praise of art from the opening of her *magnum opus*, *Metaphysics as a Guide to Morals* (8). Art is central to her moral vision, and she has added so munificently to the store of art in the world, to our great enrichment. So here, with love and gratitude for Iris Murdoch, it is:

> *A hymn of praise in gratitude for the joys and consolations and general usefulness of art might run as follows. Art is informative and entertaining, it condenses and clarifies the world, directing attention upon particular things [...] Art illuminates accident and contingency and the general muddle of life, the limitations of time and the discursive intellect, so as to enable us to survey complex or horrible things which would otherwise appal us. It creates an authoritative public human world, a treasury of past experience, it preserves the past. Art makes places and opens spaces for reflection, it is a defence against materialism and against pseudo-scientific attitudes to life. It calms and invigorates, it gives us energy by unifying, possibly by purifying, our feelings. In enjoying great art we experience a clarification and concentration and perfection of our whole consciousness. Emotion and intellect are unified into a limited whole. In this sense art also creates its client [...] The art object conveys, in the most accessible and for many the only available form, the idea of a transcendent perfection. Great art inspires us because it is separate, it is for nothing, it is for itself. It is an image of virtue. Its condensed, clarified, presentation enables us to look without sin upon a sinful world. It renders innocent and transforms into truthful vision our baser energies connected with power, curiosity, envy and sex.*

Works by Iris Murdoch

Novels

1954 *Under the Net*
1956 *The Flight from the Enchanter*
1957 *The Sandcastle*
1958 *The Bell*
1961 *A Severed Head*
1962 *An Unofficial Rose*
1963 *The Unicorn*
1964 *The Italian Girl*
1965 *The Red and the Green*
1966 *The Time of the Angels*
1968 *The Nice and the Good*
1969 *Bruno's Dream*
1970 *A Fairly Honourable Defeat*
1971 *An Accidental Man*
1973 *The Black Prince*
1974 *The Sacred and Profane Love Machine*
1975 *A Word Child*
1976 *Henry and Cato*
1978 *The Sea, the Sea*
1980 *Nuns and Soldiers*
1983 *The Philosopher's Pupil*
1985 *The Good Apprentice*
1987 *The Book and the Brotherhood*
1989 *The Message to the Planet*
1993 *The Green Knight*
1995 *Jackson's Dilemma*

Major Philosophical Writings

1953 *Sartre Romantic Rationalist*
1970 *The Sovereignty of Good*
1977 *The Fire and the Sun: Why Plato Banished the Artists*
1992 *Metaphysics as a Guide to Morals*
1997 *Existentialists and Mystics (edited by Peter Conradi)*

Parallel Sequence of Iris Murdoch's Writings During this Period

Novels	Philosophy
	1950 'The Novelist as Metaphysician'
	1950 'The Existentialist Hero'
	1951 'Thinking and Language'
	1952 'Nostalgia for the Particular'
	1952 'The Existentialist Political Myth'
	1953 *Sartre, Romantic Rationalist*
1954 *Under the Net*	
1956 *The Flight from the Enchanter*	1956 'Vision and Choice in Morality'
1957 *The Sandcastle*	

Notes

[1] Catherine Neal Parke, *Biography: Writing Lives* (New York & London: Routledge, 2002), p.32.

[2] A new biography competition for short innovative pieces designed to lead to publication by Kingston University Press Ltd.

[3] This first taxonomy of biography is taken from Erling A. Erickson, 'Biography', Vol.2. *The World Book Encyclopaedia*, 22 Vols, (Chicago: World Book, 1993) [*my arrangement of the list of items, flows on in Peake's text*].

[4] This second taxonomy of biography is taken from James L. Clifford, *From Puzzles to Portraits: Problems of a Literary Biographer* (Chapel Hill: University of North Carolina Press, 1970), 84-87 [*my arrangement of the list of items, flows on in Peake's text*].

[5] Alexandra Harris, *Virginia Woolf* (London: Thames & Hudson, 2011).

[6] Although I don't enter into dialogue with individual scholars in this book, I do want to pay tribute to Peter Conradi and Anne Rowe who have done so much to establish and maintain living engagement with her work, and who have made Kingston University the hub of the Iris Murdoch world.

[7] A long letter to Queneau explores her mistrust of psychoanalysis: 'I don't think either that this is just blind resistance or prejudice. [...] It's that I doubt the value of the thing to me – and rather fear its dangers in general. [...] What analysts do one does, ordinarily, in part for oneself – and also if one is fortunate enough to have friends who are wise and critical and loving (and I have such friends) this also can help, and change, deeply. I know that nothing in the world can be like a deep analysis – but I don't feel that it's necessarily, or even often, a "better" thing than mending one's life by the ordinary methods. [...] As to whether one can mend it by ordinary methods – I can only say that I think I can' (11 January 1953). *The Good Apprentice* (1985) explores such 'ordinary methods' of psychic healing.

[8] Jane Austen, *Love and Freindship*, (Forgotten Books, 2008), p.82.

[9] Peter J. Conradi, *Iris Murdoch: A Life* (London: HarperCollins, 2001); A.N. Wilson, *Iris Murdoch as I Knew Her* (London: Hutchinson, 2003); Valerie Purton, *An Iris Murdoch Chronology* (London: Palgrave Macmillan, 2007); David Morgan, *With Love and Rage: A Friendship with Iris Murdoch* (Kingston: Kingston University Press, 2010); Priscilla Martin and Anne Rowe, *Iris Murdoch: A Literary Life* (London: Palgrave, 2010).

[10] Cheryl Bove and Anne Rowe, *Sacred Space, Beloved City: Iris Murdoch's London* (Newcastle: Cambridge Scholars Publishing, 2008).

[11] John Bayley, *Iris* (London: Duckworth, 1998), and *Iris and the Friends* (London: Duckworth, 1998). The third volume of the trilogy, *Widower's House* (London: Duckworth, 2001), is a fantasy wrought by a mind disturbed by grief and loneliness before John Bayley's re-marriage to Audi Villiers, and it is closer in tone and substance to his curious and under-rated novels.

[12] Peter J. Conradi, ed., *Iris Murdoch: A Writer at War: Letters and Diaries 1939-45* (London: Short Books, 2010)

[13] *Living on Paper: Letters from Iris Murdoch: 1934-1995*, edited by Anne Rowe and Avril Horner (London: Chatto & Windus, forthcoming 2014).

[14] Iris Murdoch, *Under the Net* (1961); (London: Vintage, 2002), p.137.

[15] Kierkegaard, Journals IVA 164 (1843).

[16] Justin Broackes, Introduction to *Iris Murdoch, Philosopher*, ed., Justin Broackes (Oxford: Oxford University Press, 2011).

[17] Iris Murdoch, interview with Susan Hill, *Bookshelf*, BBC Radio 4, 30 April 1982.

[18] Kenneth and Margaret Thompson, *Sartre: Life and Work* (Facts on

File: New York and London, 1984), p.62.

[19] This notebook is held in the Iris Murdoch Special Collections in Kingston University Archives, IML 682.

[20] IML30 in the Iris Murdoch Special Collections.

[21] Iris Murdoch, interview with Sheila Hale, *Harpers and Queen*, 1976.

[22] KUAS70/1/115 St Anne's, 17 Feb 1952.

[23] Raymond Queneau, *Pierrot mon ami* (Paris: Gallimard, 1942). IML 85: presentation copy, inscribed on half-title 'pour Mademoiselle Iris Murdoch que ce pensum ne vous faire[?] pas oublier [Mon Ami]tié R. Queneau 25 février 1946', with the word 'Pierrot' crossed through.

[24,25] Raymond Queneau, *Journaux 1914-1965* (Paris: Gallimard, 1996), 585.

[26] Letter to Hal Lidderdale, 17 April 1946.

[27] For a full account of their relationship and their letters, see *Writer at War*, part II, 'Writing to Frank Thompson'.

[28] For a full account of their relationship and their letters, see *Writer at War*, part III, 'Writing to David Hicks'.

[29] Iris Murdoch, *A Fairly Honourable Defeat* (1970); (London: Vintage, 2001), p.55.

[30] See Anne Rowe, 'Thou art the Journey: The Sister Marian Letters, Iris Murdoch Newsletter, 19 (Autumn 2006), 22-29.

[31] N. Mackenzie, ed., *Conviction* (London:MacGibbon & Kee, 1958).

[32] Bryan Magee, *Men of Ideas: Some Creators of Contemporary Philosophy* (Oxford: Open University Press, 1982).

[33] Iris Murdoch, *Existentialists and Mystics: Writings on Philosophy and*

Literature (London: Chatto & Windus, 1997), 293.

[34] These books are held in the Iris Murdoch Collections at Kingston University Archives.

[35] Letter of commendation from John Wisdom, 26 May 1948), Newnham College Archives, item 28.

[36] Copy of Finals results sheet from J. D. Mabbott, Oxford. St Anne's College Archives.

[37] I must acknowledge the kind hospitality and helpfulness of the Newnham College Archivist, Anne Thompson, and the St Anne's College Archivist, Sally Speirs; also the help of my colleague, Alison Scott-Baumann, who shared research days (and picnics) with me. While thanking archivists, special gratitude must go to the Kingston University Archivist, Katie Giles, for her patient help with all queries during the writing of this book.

[38] Bayley, *Iris* (1998),165.

[39] Newnham College, Archives, item 1.

[40] Letter to Queneau, Chiswick, 14 July 1946.

[41] Reference from Mildred Hartley, 2 June 1946. Newnham College Archives, item 4.

[42] Reference from Donald McKinnon, 3 June 1947. Newnham College Archives, item 10.

[43] Letter to Queneau, Newnham, 5 October 1947.

[44] Letter to Queneau, Newnham, 14 October 1947.

[45] Letter to Queneau, Newnham, 15 November 1947.

[46] In no less a place than the Gifford Lectures website http://www.giffordlectures.org/Author.asp?AuthorID=131 [accessed 08-06-13]

[47] Letter to Queneau, Chiswick, 29 September 1950.

[48] Letter to Queneau, Newnham, 15 November 1947.

[49] Newnham College Archives, item 1.

[50] St Anne's College Archives.

[51] St Anne's College Archives.

[52] The Oxford University Archives, FA 9/1/219.

[53] 17 June 1999, St Anne's College Archives.

[54] Iris Murdoch, *Sartre, Romantic Rationalist* (Cambridge: Bowes & Bowes, 1953).

[55] Letter to Hal Lidderdale, unaddressed and undated.

[56] Letter to Lidderdale,18 August 1946.

[57] Broackes, 4. I am indebted to the clear overview of Iris Murdoch's impact on British philosophy at this period given in Justin Broackes's excellent Introduction to this collection.

[58] Broackes, 4.

[59] *EM*, 221.

[60] The Oxford University Archives, FA 9/1/219.

[61] *Under the Net*, pp 277-8.

[62] Preface to *Iris Murdoch: A Reassessment* ed., Anne Rowe (London: Palgrave Macmillan, 2007), xvi.

[63] You can see images from the filming of *The Bell* at http://www.memoriesofcomptonverney.org.uk/memory/searchresult.aspx?tag=Films

[64] Bayley, *Iris* (1998), 178.

[65] John Bayley, *The Characters of Love, A Study in the Literature of Personality* (London: Constable, 1960).

[66] (*EM*, 247).

[67] Peter Conradi, *The Saint and the Artist*, xvii.

[68] Letter from Henry James to Henry Adamson, 19 November 1903, 62-63, *The Correspondence of Henry James and Henry Adamson, 1877-1914*, 62, ed. George Monteiro (Baton Rouge: Lousiana State University Press, 1992), quoted in Parke, p.19.

[69] T.S. Eliot, *Complete Poems and Plays*, p.182.

[70] Letter to Queneau, 27 May 1952.

[71] William Shakespeare, *Julius Caesar*, 3:ii.

[72] Lidderdale 56, Newnham.

[73] 'Questioning Krishnamurti', *Iris Murdoch News Letter* 9 (1996).

[74] Olivia Laing, *To the River: A Journey Beneath the Surface* (London: Canongate, 2011), p.110.

[75] Peter Conradi *The Saint and the Artist*, 57.

[76] Andrew Bennett and Nicholas Royle, *Elizabeth Bowen and the Dissolution of the Novel: Still Lives* (New York & London: St Martins's Press & Macmillan, 1995), p.133.

[77] Orhan Pamuk, *Other Colours*: *Writings on Life, Art, Books and Cities*, translated by Maureen Freely (London: Faber & Faber, 2007), p.133.

Acknowledgements

Signature of Iris Murdoch taken from letter to author

Quotations from St Anne's College's archives are by kind permission of the Principal and Fellows of St Anne's College, Oxford.

Quotations from Newnham College's archives are by kind permission of the Principal and Fellows of Newnham College, Cambridge.

Quotations from the Oxford University archives are by kind permission of the Keeper of the Archives, University of Oxford, Bodleian Library.

Quotations from Kingston University archives are by kind permission of Kingston University Archives and Special Collections.

Much gratitude to is due to Peter J. Conradi and Alison Hill who read and advised on earlier drafts of the text, and saved me from many errors: all remaining errors are my own.

9 781899 999606